BLACK & BUDDHIST

What Buddhism Can Teach
Us about Race, Resilience,
Transformation & Freedom

EDITED BY
PAMELA AYO YETUNDE
& CHERYL A. GILES

FOREWORD BY
GAYLON FERGUSON

SHAMBHALA

T0036926

Shambhala Publications, Inc.
2129 13th Street
Boulder, Colorado 80302
www.shambhala.com

Cover art: Diana Ejaita
Cover and interior design: Kate E. White

9 8 7 6 5 4 3 2

Printed in the United States of America

♾ This edition is printed on acid-free paper that meets the
American National Standards Institute z39.48 Standard.
♻ This book is printed on 30% postconsumer recycled paper.
For more information please visit www.shambhala.com.
Shambhala Publications is distributed worldwide by Penguin
Random House, Inc., and its subsidiaries.

LIBRARY OF CONGRESS CATALOGING-IN-PUBLICATION DATA
Names: Yetunde, Pamela Ayo, editor. | Giles, Cheryl A., editor.
Title: Black and Buddhist: what Buddhism can teach us about race,
resilience, transformation, and freedom / edited by Pamela Ayo
Yetunde and Cheryl A. Giles; foreword by Gaylon Ferguson.
Description: First edition. | Boulder, Colorado: Shambhala, 2020.
Identifiers: LCCN 2020017025 | ISBN 9781611808650
(trade paperback)
Subjects: LCSH: Buddhism—United States. |
African Americans—Religion.
Classification: LCC BQ732 .B53 2021 | DDC 294.3089/96073—dc23
LC record available at https://lccn.loc.gov/2020017025

DEDICATION

We stand on the shoulders of African American Buddhist, dharmic, and secular mindfulness practitioners and writers who have imagined a better world and have tirelessly labored to realize their dreams for the African American community. Their words are an enduring thread of the griot tradition that now includes Buddhist-inspired liberative literature. These modern-day griots have told stories, given dharma talks, conducted research on Buddhism, and written in ways that remind us to renew cultural memory and honor the presence of ancestral voices that are with us to this day. We urge you to find their writings. Because of their pioneering work, we dedicate this book to:

Faith Adiele
Hilda Gutiérrez Baldoquin
Angela Dews
Acharya Gaylon Ferguson
Herbie Hancock
Jules Shuzen Harris
bell hooks
Charles Johnson
Sensei Alex Kakuyo
Rhonda Magee
Zenju Earthlyn Manuel
George Mumford
Lama Rod Owens
Meikle Paschal
Ralph Steele

Jasmine Syedullah
Alice Walker
Rev. angel Kyodo williams
Jan Willis

We believe there are many other African American Buddhist, dharmic, and secular mindfulness authors whose writings may not be in a book, their books have yet to see the light of day, or their books have not been as widely distributed as the authors mentioned above. We humbly ask for your forgiveness if we did not mention your book; we simply may not know your book exists.

CONTENTS

IN HONOR OF GEORGE FLOYD

PAMELA AYO YETUNDE
& CHERYL A. GILES

The chapters in this book were written many months before May 25, 2020. On that date—another one that will live in infamy in United States and international history—four Minneapolis, Minnesota, police officers participated in the public torture and killing of George Floyd, an unarmed Black man, right in front of people who begged the officers to stop. With cameras recording the scene from different angles, nearly every detail of his torture and murder was caught on tape and shown countless times on every major United States television network. The recordings went viral throughout the world and shocked humanity into action against police brutality and governmental tyranny.

George Floyd, a forty-six-year-old father of two, known to be a loving man and an advocate for gun control, was arrested for allegedly using a counterfeit twenty-dollar bill to buy cigarettes. Store employees called the police. The police arrested Floyd while he was sitting in a car, put him in handcuffs, and ultimately put him facedown on the ground while one of the officers drove his knee into Floyd's neck for nearly nine minutes. Each officer initially participated in keeping Floyd on the ground. Then, while one officer continued choking Floyd with his knee, two others kept him down as a fourth stood between the choking officer and bystanders. During those grueling eight-plus minutes, Good Samaritan bystanders repeatedly pled for mercy as the cameras captured the gruesome scene. At least one of the bystanders approached the kneeling police officer, who reached for his holster.

His hands were free to do so because his knee was on Floyd's neck while the other officers supported the commission of the torturous murder. Another Good Samaritan, concerned for the person approaching the police, warned that the officer had mace, so the bystander retreated. The cameras kept rolling.

The officer who stepped between the torturer and the bystanders repeatedly repositioned his body in an attempt to block Floyd's face and upper body from view. All the while, Floyd said repeatedly, "I can't breathe." He cried out for his mother even though she had died two years earlier. His plea seemed to be for the protection of her spirit, and perhaps it was also an announcement that he was about to join her, as his life was being choked out of him, foam spilling from his mouth onto the pavement. Floyd repeatedly said, in tones audible to those around him, that he could not breathe. The independent coroner determined Floyd died of asphyxia. Of course he had—Floyd himself testified, before several witnesses, to the cause of his death. But what caused the asphyxia was cold-blooded torture. The look on the officer's face, and the way his upper body remained relaxed, demonstrated a state of mind that seemed eerily calm. Here was a police officer using the power entrusted to him by the state to engage in a heinous, sadistic ritual with someone who had no way of resisting.

Minneapolis activists immediately called on the legal system to bring murder charges against all the officers. The mayor of Minneapolis, Jacob Frey, called for each officer to be fired. Minneapolis Police Chief Medaria Arradondo, an Afro-Latino officer, quickly fired the officers, and they were charged soon thereafter. Activists, the mayor, and the police chief were on the same page from the start regarding the officers' dismissal. In the context of the police killing of an unarmed Black person, this was unusual. The officer who choked Floyd was initially charged with third-degree murder and second-degree manslaughter. This was unusual. The murder charge was upgraded to second-degree. This was unusual. The other three officers were charged with aiding and abetting second-degree murder, as well as aiding and abetting second-degree manslaughter. This was unusual. The

State of Minnesota filed a civil rights charge against the police department. This was unusual.

Business as usual is that most police officers who kill unarmed Black people are not found guilty of any charge—even when caught on tape, and even when there are witnesses. Could the early, unusual moves toward justice for a Black man in a state as white as Minnesota be partly attributed to the fact that the Minnesota Attorney General, Keith Ellison, is a Black man? In the history of the United States there have only been eleven African American state attorneys general, and there were only six at the time of Floyd's murder. To have a Black state attorney general and a Black police chief in a largely white state and city is still unusual.

What would also be unusual, yet just, is for the police officers to be held to standards used in international human rights cases—and indeed, lawyers for Floyd's family have announced that they will take the case to the United Nations Human Rights Commission. Why? Floyd's eight-plus minutes of torture and murder "shocked the conscience" of humanity, transcending race, city, state, and nation. Protests throughout the world took place for at least three weeks. Human rights advocate Rev. Al Sharpton, who officiated Floyd's funerals, called on people to march on Washington, DC, on August 28, 2020, the fifty-seventh anniversary of the 1963 March on Washington, where Rev. Dr. Martin Luther King Jr. gave his iconic "I Have a Dream" speech.

As we wrote this preface in early June 2020, protests occurred in cities, suburbs, and towns throughout the United States. Beginning in Minneapolis and Saint Paul, the protests expanded to include other cities such as Atlanta; Bakersfield, California; Boston; Chicago; Columbus, Ohio; Dallas, Houston, and Fort Worth; Denver; Des Moines; Detroit; Los Angeles; Louisville, Kentucky; Memphis; New York City; Philadelphia; Phoenix; Pittsburg; Portland; Sacramento; Salt Lake City; San Jose; Seattle; several cities throughout North Carolina; Washington, DC; and other places. The protests were a mixture of nonviolence and violence, constructive calls for justice and destructive behaviors against property. Overall, they were thoroughly racially and culturally diverse.

Those protesting violence were sometimes met with governmental violence, especially at night. For example, in Louisville, Kentucky, during a protest against police brutality on May 29, seven people were shot by local police. Two months earlier, on March 13, Breonna Taylor, an EMT and unarmed Black woman, was killed by police after they barged into her apartment with a "no knock" warrant. They shot her eight times.

Taylor's murder took place about three months before Floyd was choked to death. About a month before that, a white father and son vigilante pair (with the aid of another white man who videotaped the shooting) shot and killed an unarmed Black man, Ahmaud Arbery, while he was jogging in Brunswick, Georgia. Did the killings of Arbery and Taylor help give rise to the scale of the response to Floyd's murder? The rage had been building for decades, and the provocations of that rage did not stop with Floyd. As justice watchers were trying to get a handle on what happened to Floyd and what happened in the aftermath of his death, the Austin, Texas police department released a video of police officers arresting and tasing to death yet another Black man, Javier Ambler. Other such videos are now coming to light all over the country.

Time will tell whether the unusual moves toward justice in Minnesota will effectuate long-lasting change, but in the meantime, protests have spread throughout the world because the brutal policing of people of color is actually an international phenomenon. As the worldwide protests swelled, so did President Donald J. Trump's fear.

Trump threatened to shoot and unleash dogs on protesters, harkening back to the 1960s, Bull Connor–style way of policing protestors. Trump's threats, though not veiled, were also code to his white supremacist supporters that he was still with them. He was called out for using racist tropes. He accused governors of being weak because they did not use excessive force to dominate protestors, and he demanded they do so, and do so quickly. The National Guard was dispatched to twenty-five states and Washington, DC. Protestors took their grievances as close to the

White House as they could get. Trump ordered 32,000 United States military troops to occupy thirty-two states, and he ordered barriers be placed around the White House to protect him from the growing number of protestors outside what is otherwise known as The People's House. Trump's presidential legacy was unraveled, and so was he.

Trump got his wall, though it turned out not to be on the border but rather between him and an intergenerational rainbow coalition of activists—a coalition tired of business as usual and inspired by the likes of Senator Bernie Sanders and Rev. Jessie Jackson. We believe Rev. Dr. King would have cried tears of joy to see the beloved community of which he dreamed marching arm-in-arm toward freedom from tyranny.

People took to the streets to express their outrage at the police killings of Floyd, Taylor, Arbery, and told and untold other Black Americans. The videotaped police beating of Rodney King occurred in 1991; setting aside the issue of racist cops in fictional movies and television shows, the nation had been watching broadcasts of real Black people beaten and killed by real police officers for twenty-nine years! A generation had grown up knowing they could be murdered by a police officer, have the murder videotaped, have the videotape shown throughout the world, and justice would not be served. Police brutality against Black people is an existential situation unlike any other, so the protests continued, even in a pandemic that disproportionately affected African American and Latinx communities.

Hundreds of thousands of people defied curfews and social distancing guidelines in order to protest, even as the COVID-19 pandemic continued. In the United States, we surpassed two million (and rising) people infected with 116,000 (and rising) dead, and over forty million (and rising) people unemployed. In the world, nearly eight million (and rising) people were infected with 434,000 (and rising) dead. Our lives, loved ones, and economies were devastated, all in a matter of five months. With the United States' retaliatory withdrawal from the World Health Organization

(WHO), no coordinated national or international plan was in sight. Yet, we were not entirely defined by this devastation.

More people took to the streets in protest than COVID-19 took lives. Though there was no COVID-19 vaccine, there were horizontal and vertical measures taken to dismantle and destruct symbols of anti-Blackness. These included lowering and removing Confederate flags from Army, Marine, and Navy bases as well as the National Association for Stock Car Auto Racing (NASCAR); removing and defacing statues of slaveholding Confederate leaders; and attempts to remove the names of anti-Black military officers from United States military bases. Activists turned their sorrow over Floyd's death into proposals to defund police departments. To "defund," in this context, refers to a host of possible measures. These exist on a spectrum from ending conventional police departments and replacing them with community-led models to reallocating resources from police departments to other government agencies—such as those that focus on health care, mental health care, food security, and homelessness—that enhance a community's chances of living more abundantly. Democrats and Republicans began crafting policing reform bills. Even the country music group Lady Antebellum changed its name to Lady A. (In the US context, *antebellum* refers to the pre-Civil War era, when chattel slavery was practiced throughout the South.) The cultural shifts were swift and wide, and like other cultural shifts, they will take time to fasten and deepen.

In the meantime, we stand in solidarity with those who protest against police killings and seek justice for George Floyd and the many others who have been killed, and whose killings are being revealed. We know that silence only ensures that the violence against Black and brown bodies by white supremacy will continue to render more violence until we are all dead. We will not be silent. This country began with a clarion call by the Founding Fathers to "Live Free or Die" as they sought their freedom and independence by shaping a nation built on democracy. They chose to rebel and protect their freedom rather than be dominated by Great Britain. We have been seeking our freedom from domination of white supremacy for more than four hundred years. Our humanity and right to live requires that we act to protect our lives, and so we resist. We know that resistance is in the blood of America and "freedom through violence is a privilege possessed only by whites."* With that understanding, we know our actions will be criticized and seen as un-American or unpatriotic at best. Many will demonize us for taking action. Yet, we know we must stand up and that without rebellion or resistance, change will not happen and we cannot survive.

Recognizing our deepest feelings, we know we cannot live fully with suffering, invisibility, and dehumanization. Our resistance to oppression is our right to breathe freely, without the force of a hand or foot or knee on our throats constantly draining the life out of us. By watching Black and brown bodies die by police violence without resistance, we slowly die too. We take in resignation, despair, depression, self-denial, and self-effacement, and our bodies become bloated with powerlessness. And perhaps by not resisting, we unwittingly make a choice to allow ourselves to be silenced because we are too afraid to claim and honor the most precious gift we hold: the breath. But as Black Buddhist practitioners, we intimately know the breath through mindfulness of the breath. In honor of George Floyd and countless others, we vow to breathe. We breathe for the well-being of all sentient beings.

As is common in many Buddhist communities, we end this preface with a "dedication of the merit." In short, a dedication of the merit is an aspiration to use the gifts of Buddhist practice—generosity, virtue, renunciation, wisdom, energy, patience, truthfulness, resolve, lovingkindness, and equanimity—not for ourselves, but for others. This dedication of merit was written by Sosan Theresa Flynn, Zen Priest and Guiding Teacher of Clouds in Water Zen Center in St. Paul, Minnesota. It was recited on Sunday, June 7, 2020:

* Kellie Carter Jackson, "The Double Standard of the American Riot," *The Atlantic*, accessed June 3, 2020, https://www.theatlantic.com/culture/archive/2020/06/riots-are-american-way-george-floyd-protests/612466/.

Leader: Our brother George Floyd, your life was full and not without difficulties. You needlessly died as a direct result of racism. May your friends and family and all those who mourn your death, the protesters demonstrating for a better world and society, the police officers involved in your death, the white supremacists and all those whose pain causes them to tear things down, the people who are afraid, those who are angry, those who are hopeless, all humans, non-humans and the great earth itself—may we all be supported deeply in the dharma, be peaceful and free from suffering, and may we, together with all beings, realize Buddha's way.

The clear, refreshing moon of Wisdom and Compassion shines freely in the sky of absolute emptiness. When the minds of ordinary beings are pure, the moon's reflection appears. George Floyd, on May 25, 2020, the karmic bonds that held you to this world were extinguished and your great life suddenly came to an end. At this very moment, may the merit of this chant extinguish the fire of inexhaustible ignorance so that by the manifestation of subtle, perfect wisdom you may realize the truth and enter nirvana with joy.

All: All Buddhas throughout space and time
All honored ones, bodhisattvas, mahasattvas
Wisdom beyond wisdom, mahaprajnaparamita.

With this chant, Clouds in Water Zen Center dedicated George Floyd to the saints, the cloud of witnesses, the pantheon of protectors, and into mahaprajnaparamita—the wisdom beyond wisdom.

FOREWORD

Being Black Buddhists: Liberation, Suffering, and Celebration

GAYLON FERGUSON

Let me begin this foreword by inviting you to a feast. The eight bold chapters gathered here are a feast of inspiration and insight, tenderness and truth, courage and compassion. These sisters and brothers on the path of awakening—these authors—have prepared a delicious feast for all of us to enjoy as we are nourished and strengthened in love. I am so grateful to all of them for what they offer us here. Their stories and teachings are a generous offering of genuine lovingkindness. I bow gratefully to all their teachers and their teachers' teachers, and all the ancestors who have worked hard to pass on to us a precious path to complete awakening.

Now, more than ever, we need this message of peace, a strong peace with justice and dignity. This is a practical message of cultivating inner spiritual power to meet the daily challenges of aggression, violence, lying, and deception. We are all thirsty and hungry for the beautiful message of truth. As Stevie Wonder "the Wonder man" sings, "Love's in need of love today." Reminding us of the value of inner treasures of the spirit, Dr. Martin Luther King Jr. warned: "We have foolishly minimized the internal of our lives and maximized the external." Here, then, is an alternative to the widely available, false, and numbing paths used to avoid our experiences of fear, anxiety, worry, and despair. When we turn toward (rather than away from) whatever arises in our lives, our strength and resilience grow and expand like the branches of a vast, immovable tree with deep roots.

This fresh feast offering makes available to us, during a speedy and confusing time, the ancient knowledge and wisdom of the Indian sage known as "Buddha," awakened one. One of the awakened one's wise sayings points directly to the freedom which is at the heart of all these practices and teachings: "Just as the great ocean has one taste, the taste of salt, so also this teaching has one taste, the taste of liberation." Liberating ourselves and others is the courageous heart of this path. As Lama Rod Owens writes in his chapter here, "I will start by admitting that the only thing I have ever wanted is to be free. I grew up in the Black church where we were very interested in freedom. One of the stories that we all knew by heart was the Exodus." Reading these eight essays, I've been reminded again and again of our great love of freedom. We want freedom—for ourselves, for our families and communities, for our people, for all beings. What is at the root of this strong motivation, this powerful desire for complete liberation? The Buddhist teacher Suzuki Roshi called this our "inmost request." Deep down, this is what we human beings want most in this life.

Black liberation theology reminds us: true freedom has both outer and inner dimensions. In her amazingly graceful memoir, *Dreaming Me: Black, Baptist, and Buddhist*, Professor Jan Willis tells the story of meeting her Tibetan teacher Lama Yeshe for the first time in Asia. He asked, "Now, please tell me, why have you come?" On the spot, Willis gave a somewhat general, textbook-correct answer, but then reflected later, "I should have told him the truth when he'd first asked; should have blurted out that I suffered; that I was often frustrated and angry; that slavery and its legacy of racism had taken its toll on me; that I had come seeking help in coping with feelings of inadequacy, unworthiness, and shame."[1] Well said. As the author Charles Johnson phrases it, "The black experience in America, like the teachings of Shakyamuni Buddha, begins in suffering."[2] As descendants of brutally enslaved Africans, we are passionately committed and deeply devoted to personal and communal healing and freedom.

FREEDOM STORIES

There are moving stories of personal, familial, and communal history in every chapter of this book. Our lives and the lives of those who've been here before us—our mothers, fathers, sisters, and brothers—are all threads joined together in one garment, a single destiny. These stories show a unified path joining ordinary, everyday life with transformative spiritual practices, continuing the same personal and collective journeys toward complete liberation that we've been making for centuries. We, as a people, will get there.

Cheryl Giles begins her chapter "They Say the People Could Fly" by contemplating American history: "The legacy of black enslaved bodies is a powerful example of the enduring spirit of resistance and love that serves as a reminder that freedom is possible." Using Virginia Hamilton's version of a black American folktale of Ibo people flying away to freedom, she connects the deeper meanings of this symbolic story with the painful yet necessary work of remembering the horrors of our past. "With freedom came the awakening that the end of suffering was possible. Drawing upon the metaphor of flight as a tool for liberation, 'The People Could Fly' and other folktales demonstrate the resilience of slaves in finding freedom and safety for themselves and others." These ancestral stories encode and transmit an indestructible message for us: we can find a better place, a different way of being. "Way above the plantations, way over the slavery land. Say they flew away to Free-dom."

In "From Butcher to Zen Priest," Gyōzan Royce Andrew Johnson tells the story of the big changes in his life that led to his embrace of the meditation path and way of life of Zen Buddhism. He shares with us the moving and dramatic story of a life-changing day he almost bled to death: "This day was the beginning of my renunciation of butchering dead animals for human consumption and my transformation toward becoming a Zen priest." This is another journey to realizing freedom.

For Gyōzan, making this spiritual journey meant facing nervousness, fear, and anxiety as part of an inward-facing path of knowing himself in a deeper and more complete way. "Some months after I accidentally cut myself, I was sitting in the passenger seat of my friend's car while he took me to my first meditation sitting. . . . I hardly knew anything about mindfulness meditation, but I was willing to go despite the fact that I was nervous about it. The closer we got to the meditation center, the more anxious I became. . . . What was I afraid of? My nervousness, I believe, stemmed from a near-conscious acknowledgment that I had a lot of mental work to do and that work would require me looking at uncomfortable and unpleasant places of the mind. I knew it needed to be done, but I felt fear about exploring uncharted territory." Reading Gyōzan's description of his challenging journey, I often wondered why a person would commit to such rigorous training. Clearly, it's not an easy journey. What shows through here is strong commitment to a path that leads to liberation.

Ruth King builds her chapter "Wholeness Is No Trifling Matter" around the earliest teachings of the Buddha, the Four Noble Truths: (1) there is suffering, (2) there is a cause of suffering, (3) there is freedom from suffering, and (4) there is a path to this freedom. She quotes the wisdom of President Nelson Mandela: "When we can sit in the face of insanity or dislike and be free from the need to make it different, then we are free." In King's spiritual journey, mindfulness and insight meditations were keys to discovering this inner freedom. "Through meditation practice, I was beginning to realize that my mind—my relationship to distress— was not only a righteous and persistent oppressor but also my understanding of the nature of mind was my ticket to freedom."

In "Voluntary Segregation," Pamela Ayo Yetunde explores the self-knowledge and freedom she found practicing in, first, predominantly white *sanghas* (Buddhist communities) and then in meditation communities for people of color. "With the exception of that one instance of resistance, the whole of my experiences with white sanghas had been affirming—but that was in the San Francisco Bay Area in the early 2000s." When she moves to Atlanta, she experiences two other practice communities marked by racist microaggressions and other demeaning behaviors. Still, as a person committed to a spiritual path of awakening, she *uses* these difficulties as opportunities for self-inquiry and learning by moving beyond familiar yet confining habitual patterns of always seeking comfort: "I did the unexpected. I decided to stay where I felt unwelcome by some. . . . I discovered I wasn't dependent on them to teach me Zen, but I sat with them to understand something about myself. I found I could practice the dharma in a community that I was not dependent on for teachings. . . . These realizations had implications for my off-the-cushion life as well." This is an example of using rocks in the road as stepping stones to discover unconditional, inner freedom.

On the other hand, Yetunde's practice within people of color sanghas brings forward other liberating forms of being together. "By sitting together, POC may experience a variety of forms of secular and spiritual liberation; to be liberated in any of these forms promotes the ability to be in solidarity with others." She is particularly insightful in articulating the necessity and the benefits of meditating in these practice communities: "Paradoxically, transforming the delusion of separation may also need to happen in a POC sangha. . . . I realize what we want to talk about in our voluntary segregation is our experiences of being 'othered,'" treated as less than human. She also writes, "POC need healing containers to talk about these lifetimes of repeated experiences without encountering opposition as we do so."

In "On Being Lailah's Daughter," Kamilah Majied has written a beautiful praise-song for her mother, clearly her first spiritual teacher. She shares a story from her childhood of being frightened for no particular reason. Mother skillfully guides daughter to find her own inner strength: "She directed me to seek out wisdom and solace myself, thus training me to grow my seeking mind, my mind of faith, throughout my life." Reading this story, I felt, *What a great gift!* This is a vivid example of ancestors guiding us, showing us the way to spacious freedom: look over *here*, not over *there*.

Sebene Selassie, an Insight Meditation teacher, narrates her own liberating journey in "Turning toward Myself." There are many twists and turns on the sometimes bumpy road to freedom: "My relationships with Blackness and Buddhism have been complex, even fraught, but often profound. Buddhism allows me to see the ever-changing being that I am. Blackness assures me that there is a glorious ancestry within me. They both espouse joy and freedom."

Selassie shows us what meditative inquiry looks like by slowly thinking through the knots and tangles of multiple, intersecting identities. "Blackness and Buddhism teach me to love my multiplicities, to love myself." She calls out the seductive and destructive pull of white supremacy: "I understand how racism teaches you to turn away from yourself. I did it for years. Turning toward myself required study and practice." This is the explosively liberating potential of these awakening teachings and practices. We can free ourselves from the mental prisons inculcated by a racist society and culture. As Bob Marley reminded us, "None but ourselves can free our minds."

A crucial part of Selassie's journey was reading and learning from the feminist wisdom teachings of Toni Morrison, Audre Lorde, bell hooks, and others. For Selassie, these writers sparked an inner revolution when she combined their writings with the powerful spiritual teachings we call *buddhadharma*, the way of awakening. "I turned toward Buddhism and Blackness at the same time. I am forever grateful for that synchronicity." Turning and turning away from oppressive structures and habits of denial of the truth of our experience, while turning toward ourselves with respect and love—this is the way. "Buddhism taught me to embrace every part of myself. That's what the dharma invites—a turning toward the truth of this body."

In a quick summary of the essence of the Four Noble Truths, Selassie writes: "One of the primary teachings I have understood from the dharma is not to be in contention with reality. This is a core teaching for liberation. Suffering (*dukkha*) comes from wanting things to be other than what they are. . . . But what if we don't see things as they are but only as we've been taught to see them?" Here Selassie is bravely leading us, by way of a seriously funny episode from Donald Glover's award-winning television series *Atlanta*, in a deeper inquiry into the idea of "race" itself. "We know race is a construct, an invention of racism. Race was created to justify imperialism and the slave trade. Blackness is not intrinsic to anyone. Blackness is definitely not monolithic. Yet, Blackness—entwined with the enslavement of Africans, colonization of the continent, and the subjugation of a massive diaspora—has become an indelible concept."

These are very deep waters to fathom, beyond simple and sometimes confining binary concepts of "she" and "he," "white" and "black." I'm reminded of a statement in an interview by Rev. angel Kyodo williams, one of the authors of *Radical Dharma: Talking Race, Love, and Liberation*. Responding to an interviewer's question about her journey, Kyodo Sensei says, "Queerness gave me the language for everything I know about liberation and freedom."

In "Belong," Lama Dawa Phillips invites us into the great vision of freeing all beings as a guiding north star shining constantly before us. "The promise of the dharma is universal liberation for all, regardless of origin, race, gender, religion, or sexual orientation. One of the reasons dharma appeals to so many minorities is its focus on liberation from struggle, pain, and suffering." Phillips connects this freedom with letting go of any and all fixed identifications: "I believe that the liberated mind has no color at all. I believe that in our heart of hearts, we are neither black nor brown, neither yellow nor white, nor pink or any other color. In our liberated mind, we are free; we are beyond color."

This is dangerous territory with many pitfalls and sidetracks all around us, so we must walk carefully here. In the pioneering collection, *Dharma, Color, and Culture*, edited by the Zen priest Ryumon Sensei (Hilda Gutiérrez Baldoquin), Jan Willis begins her chapter "Dharma Has No Color" by placing it as a response to a question from a young black woman in the closing session of the 2002 African American Buddhist Retreat and Conference at Spirit Rock Meditation Center. Contemplating these writings from Selassie and Phillips and Willis, I wondered: Does the dharma have color or no color? Both or neither?

Phillips hastens to explain, "I am not suggesting that it is not deeply important and meaningful to own our ethnic heritage or to heal all the shame and resistance to fully inhabiting ourselves. It is both critical and essential." (As we have just read, Selassie and many of us would strongly agree.) "But, on the path to greater liberation, one challenging part comes in allowing yourself to release your identification with your color and race." What is this challenge, and how might we navigate it skillfully? What is full personal and collective healing from intergenerational trauma? These are questions to be lived into, not solved through mere concepts and more ideas. Healing has to be *real*.

In "The Dharma of Trauma," Lama Rod Owens shows us how things look from a slightly different perspective. In September 2019, he attended a plant medicine retreat in Peru, led by his "homegirl and fellow dharma teacher, Spring Washam." These ayahuasca ceremonies are profoundly transformative and full of creativity. The playfully wise West African trickster spirit Anansi even made an appearance. Clearly the spiritual presences of our African ancestral deities are still with us, just waiting for us to open the door of invitation.

Owens brilliantly evokes the night-sea journeys of three ayahuasca ceremonies and the teachings he received there. "I want my Blackness to be supported by my dharma practice, not erased by it. I think that this was one of the teachings I was supposed to understand from the ceremonies." Spacious appreciation allows us to release narrow fixation while simultaneously embracing all that we are. This is true freedom.

OF SORROW SONGS AND
THE MUSIC OF CELEBRATION

In 1903, the pioneering, radical Black scholar W. E. B. Du Bois published a collection of essays of major significance, *The Souls of Black Folk*. More than a century later, we pay homage to him here as one of our great ancestors. Du Bois showed us the way. The fourteenth and final chapter of that book begins: "They that walked in darkness sang songs in the olden days—Sorrow Songs—for they were weary at heart." Du Bois recognized and valued the deep, soulful expressiveness of spirituals. These songs, he wrote, exist "as the most beautiful expression of human experience born this side of the seas."[3] Lama Rod Owens, in his chapter here, writes, "I remember the sorrow songs. 'Sorrow song'—when I first heard this phrase, a sadness came over me, and I began to shiver. It was something I couldn't articulate." Music moves us in this realm beyond words. We hear and feel and understand. Let me conclude this foreword by noting the importance of African American music in many of these stories of spiritual journeys toward freedom. Music leads us into joy and celebration. After all, what kind of feast would it be without singing some songs and dancing?

Our music, as Amiri Baraka showed long ago in *Blues People*, is essential to how we survived, how we got over, and how we made a way where there was no way. Our music, which matches our experience and history, is filled with sorrow and joy, suffering and celebration. I speak here of *all* our music—from field hollers and work songs to gospel, from Delta blues to Chicago, from bebop to hip-hop. Think of second lining and New Orleans jazz funerals. On the long, slow walk with the casket to the graveyard, the musicians begin by playing sad songs of mourning. Then, on the way back home, they switch to up-tempo music for dancing in the streets. Ralph Ellison described the artistic alchemy of the impulse to sing and play the blues: "The blues is an impulse to keep the painful details and episodes of a brutal experience alive in one's aching consciousness, to finger its jagged grain, and to transcend it, not by the consolation of philosophy but by squeezing from it a near-tragic, near-comic lyricism."[4] We cry, and we laugh, and sometimes in our music we remember them both together. My first Buddhist meditation teacher translated an important feeling term from Tibetan as "sad-joy." Black studies theorist Fred Moten shares a related insight from jazz composer and trumpeter Ishmael Wadada Leo Smith: "This is why, as Wadada Leo Smith has said, it hurts to play this music. The music is a riotous solemnity, a terrible beauty. It hurts so much that we have to celebrate. That we have to celebrate is what hurts so much."

Kamilah Majied describes her mother ("Umie") meditating on the bittersweet beauty of Lady Day's voice: "I would watch Umie listening to 'Good Morning Heartache' by Billie Holiday, with a whimsical look on her face, shaking her head as she sang the lyrics. Little did I know, as a child, that this was a meditation practice wherein my mother used the music to guide her in reconciling with the fact that sadness often wakes up with us and in us in the morning." Majied hears a key teaching from her mother on the spacious house of meditation this way: "I was young, but I got the message. Since sorrow and anxiety are part of our human experience, part of what flows through our minds constantly, we might as well make friends with [them] and learn to soothe them rather than trying to throw them out of the house of our minds." This is the central, meditative wisdom of making friends with ourselves just as we are, however we are—good days and bad days, happy feelings and sad feelings, many thoughts and few thoughts, all included, welcomed even. Majied summarizes the insight carried in singing songs of sorrow: "To me, 'Good Morning Heartache,' and many other songs my mother sang, said, 'What if we were to turn toward the sadness and welcome it?' To appreciate the part of ourselves that is still hopeful enough to *get* sad and worry. Some of us are hurt beyond sadness or worry. Some of us are stuck in rage, despair, or some pretense that everything is cool. When we can feel sadness or worry, it means we are whole and connected to our hearts." This is beautifully said, another praise-song to full human-heartedness.

Ruth King's mother was the choir director and pianist at their church in Los Angeles. On the third Friday night of each month, she held improvisational jazz sessions in the living room of their home. King tells us, bringing us right into the scene: "My mom would often hum a rhythm before expressing it on the piano and then everyone else would join in when they felt so moved—when they knew they could add value, meaning, interest, and harmony. I'd be amazed at how everything was made more powerful in ensemble. There was a sense of complementarity, not competition, as if they knew they were in cocreation and that something subtle and mysterious was unfolding. These folks were playing for each other, and there was deep respect and trust in what unfolded. No one contributed just to be heard but rather to create something more beautiful." Isn't this example of collective creativity a shining demonstration of what one Buddhist teacher called "creating enlightened society"?

King offers this as an example of those called bodhisattvas, those who are living for the well-being and awakening and liberation of all beings. She reflects on this "mysterious and precious transmission through improvisational jazz." At jazz concerts I've attended, sometimes someone who is moved by the spiritual power of the music will shout out, "*Ashe!*" That's what I want to say now: *Ashe! Ashe* for Ruth King's mother and the other musicians! King says that she asks herself daily, "As a bodhisattva, how might I see all life as art, as ceremony in service to greater well-being for all, without exception?"

So, the truth of suffering, remembering the violence and struggles of our histories and intergenerational trauma, is inseparable from rejoicing in the vision of us all being free at last. This is rejoicing in the truth of the path. Again and again, in these wonderful chapters, we hear songs of sad-joy and sweet celebration at finding the path to liberation. "When I heard that message, saw the truth so clearly, met that person who was a true spiritual friend—I felt the doors to liberation swing wide open."

When we connect with each other in truth and compassion, we also feel a connection with our ancestors. Cheryl Giles tells a story of taking a walk with Lama Rod Owens at the end of a group meditation retreat. "I was anxious about making myself vulnerable to someone I hardly knew." Bravely, she blurts out something about her inner struggle, and then asks a question about whether meditation could really make a difference. "Without hesitation, he spoke in a soft voice about the impact of intergenerational trauma on black and brown bodies, and encouraged me to sit every day. . . . He listened to me; I knew he was familiar with my struggle . . . [and] found freedom." This, too, is a sorrow song that is also a song of joy: "Whenever I feel stuck, I return to these words of wisdom that connect me to a powerful lineage of ancestors."

There are guided meditation practices at the end of the first two chapters here, as well as contemplative reflection questions in many of the essays. If you feel so inclined, please join in the feast. You are always welcome.

ACKNOWLEDGMENTS

PAMELA AYO YETUNDE

When I was a financial consultant in 2000, a friend and colleague, Rattan Dodeja, gave me a copy of Stephen Mitchell's version of the Tao Te Ching. When I finally got around to reading it, I instantly experienced peace of mind! Little did I know that the Tao Te Ching would be my preparation and introduction to the nondualism espoused in the Vietnamese Zen Buddhist monk Thich Nhat Hanh's book *Touching Peace*, given to me in 2001 by my friend and a food writer, Dianne Jacob. Two years later, Eric Poche invited me to be a bedside volunteer with Zen Hospice Project in San Francisco. I'm grateful to Rattan, Dianne, and Eric for giving me what I needed to move into a new consciousness.

Since 2000, I have been supported by many Buddhist practitioners and communities including Community of Mindful Living sangha members and teachers (particularly Lyn Fine); Spirit Rock Meditation Center teachers (particularly Gil Fronsdal) and retreats; Sati Center for Buddhist Studies Chaplaincy Program taught by Gil Fronsdal, Jennifer Block, Paul Haller, and Diana Lion; Spirit Rock's Community Dharma Leaders program taught by Eugene Cash, Gina Sharpe, Thanissara, and Larry Yang; the Shambhala Atlanta People of Color sangha (especially Brenda Collins); and the Twin Cities Minnesota dharma communities, including Clouds in Water Zen Center, Common Ground Meditation Center, and Minnesota Zen Meditation Center. I have made lasting friendships in all these programs. Thank you, friends!

Three Christian theologians, Pamela Cooper-White, Emmanuel Lartey, and Beverly Wallace, and one Christian theologian who practices Buddhism, Duane Bidwell, supported my dissertation on African-descended lesbian Buddhist practitioners while I was at Columbia Theological Seminary. It was not lost on me how unusual it was to write about a population most seminarians do not write about, but to have the support of these august scholars was priceless. To all these Buddhist practitioners, Christian pastoral theologians, and Buddhist and Christian educational programs, including University of the West and Upaya Institute and Zen Center, I am grateful for a consciousness that is more thoroughly East-West integrated.

Charlotte Collins, Koun Franz, and Melvin McLeod, the editors of *American Buddhist Women, Buddhadharma,* and *Lion's Roar,* respectively, have published my writings. Thank you for helping me share my thoughts and ideas. The feedback from their readers affirms the publication and "promise" of this book, which is that Buddhist practices in the transformation of suffering can heal the particular suffering of racism in the United States.

My network of African-descended Buddhist practitioners has grown exponentially due to the community-organizing work of Noliwe Alexander, Myokei Caine-Barrett, Konda Mason, and Rev. angel Kyodo williams. The Gathering II conference that took place in October 2019 was truly life-changing; I could see evidence of and be embraced by a dynamic community of Black wellness I had not viscerally experienced before. A real Wakanda!

Before that Wakanda experience, The Gathering I conference took place at Union Theological Seminary in 2018. After that conference, I was contacted by Shambhala Publications to consider writing a book, and here it is! This book would not be but for one of Shambhala's editors, Matt Zepelin, who is thoughtful, insightful, timely, and cooperative; our book's contributors Acharya Gaylon Ferguson, Gyōzan Royce Andrew Johnson, Ruth King, Kamilah Majied, Lama Rod Owens, Lama Dawa Tarchin Phillips, Sebene Selassie; and my coeditor, Cheryl A. Giles.

Cheryl is my mentor and friend. She mentored me during my postdoctoral fellowship at Harvard Divinity School, and became my friend thereafter. She has been truly enjoyable to work with. I wish all coeditors the camaraderie of mission, integrity, humor, and attentiveness that Cheryl offered me.

I am also grateful to have had the opportunity to befriend and learn from Roshi Joan Halifax, founder of Upaya Zen Center's Buddhist Chaplaincy Training Program. Here's a shoutout to cohorts eleven, twelve, and thirteen!

There is not enough space to thank everyone who played a part in the manifestation of this book, and I'm sorry about that. I do want to acknowledge the Baileys, Gambles, Halls, Matlocks, Pinners, and Scotts; my daughter, Karen; and my spouse, Tracey Scott. Tracey has supported me in practically everything I've done. Most of what I've done, since meeting her, I could not have done without her. Immeasurable gratitude to you, Tracey.

CHERYL GILES

There are many people who contributed to making this book possible, but unfortunately it is not possible to name everyone.

Pamela Ayo Yetunde, my coeditor, has my deep and abiding gratitude for her vision of this book as an opportunity to increase the visibility of Buddhism and its influence on the lives of ordinary African American folks.

Acharya Gaylon Ferguson, Gyōzan Royce Andrew Johnson, Ruth King, Kamilah Majied, Lama Rod Owens, Lama Dawa Tarchin Phillips, and Sebene Selassie—Black Buddhist teachers and leaders whose narratives speak to the suffering we all experience—have my heartfelt thanks for their contributions. By bearing witness to injustice and oppression, you all share a vision for living, loving, and building a just world.

Matt Zepelin, our editor at Shambhala Publications, was a collaborative partner who gave the project the space to unfold naturally. His insight, thoughtfulness, and generosity provided a stress-free process.

Katy Klutznick, my writing coach, generously read multiple drafts of my chapter and gave me valuable feedback. Her coaching has sustained me through this project and many others.

Lama Willa Miller, my friend and dharma teacher at Natural Dharma Fellowship, first believed we could write a book together based on the deep conversations we shared about Buddhist pastoral care in 2010. These conversations later morphed into coediting *The Arts of Contemplative Care: Pioneering Voices in Buddhist Chaplaincy and Pastoral Work*, published by Wisdom Publications in 2012.

My gratitude to the students at Harvard Divinity School whom I have taught and mentored since 1997. Their appreciation for learning has deepened my knowledge, compassion, and relational wisdom and made me a better teacher.

My heartfelt gratitude to Julie Gillette, my close colleague and friend, whose quiet leadership and compassion has deepened my love of studying the dharma.

My dear friend Hara Klein has refused to let me hide and supported me through every challenge small and large. Her commitment to justice and equity gives me hope that we can change the world.

Deep bow to Barbara Mandelkorn, my mentor, who carefully guided me to welcome and love all parts.

I am eternally grateful to Jewel Gilbert, my life partner, who has fearlessly walked the path with me and has generously given her time to support my writing and teaching.

To the legacy of my ancestors, bending and twisting to pick cotton, I offer deep gratitude. May you be blessed. My charge is to pass it forward.

BLACK AND BUDDHIST

INTRODUCTION

Buddhism as a Path of Trauma Resilience for Anti-Racism Activists

PAMELA AYO YETUNDE & CHERYL A. GILES

Buddhism is a way of life, a philosophy, a psychology, a set of ethics, a religion, or a combination thereof. Central to the many ways Buddhism is understood is the achievement of emotional, mental, and psychological wellness. African Americans are at perpetual risk of psychological imbalance and trauma due to the social realities of racism in the United States. What could Buddhism offer African Americans who want to be emotionally resilient in a context they cannot singlehandedly change?

Many African Americans who grew up learning little about Buddhism (and perhaps mostly associated it with Asians or with white Americans) may find it surprising to think of Buddhism as pertinent to their lives and struggles. Yet the roots of the tradition show us that's exactly what it is! Buddhism emerged from a caste-oriented culture in which a powerful man of color renounced his power, woke up to his delusions, grew in compassion, and committed himself to teaching a way of life for all to awaken. His teachings, at their root, were caste-disorienting. In other words, Buddhism is a path to de-caste or decolonize one's mind while simultaneously helping oneself build resilience against trauma.

More than twenty-five hundred years ago, near what is now the border of India and Nepal, a system of mental wellness was being developed to support oppressed people's desire to live with more freedom, happiness, and balance. The system is now called the Noble Eightfold Path (referred to as "the Path" hereafter), and studies have shown that implementing the Path supports psychospiritual resilience against prejudice, oppression, alienation, and trauma. What is the Path?

To understand the path, it helps to understand the four conclusions the economically and politically privileged Siddhartha Gautama (the historical man of color who became known as the Buddha, "the awakened one") came to after years of undertaking ascetic practices to try to avoid human frailty:

1. Suffering is real and shared throughout humanity.
2. There are discernable causes for this suffering.
3. These causes can be transformed and terminated.
4. The way to transform and terminate the causes is through the path.

This fourfold formula is known in Buddhism as the Four Noble Truths, referred to as Truths hereafter. The last Truth is divided into an eight-part system: Right View, Right Intention, Right Speech, Right Action, Right Livelihood, Right Effort, Right Mindfulness, and Right Concentration. In this introduction, we describe what each aspect of the Eightfold Path means, and can mean, for African Americans as they engage in anti-racist work and in the necessary struggle to maintain their own well-being.

WHAT DOES IT MEAN TO BE NOBLE AND RIGHT?

Siddhartha Gautama (also referred to as Shakyamuni Buddha in some Buddhist traditions—there are many) was born into a ruling caste and family. To be of a ruling caste means you are, conventionally speaking, considered "noble"—above and apart from the ruled castes. The formerly noble Buddha proclaimed that nobility is not about caste but is about how one lives one's life to awaken from ignorance, hatred, and greed. This was a profound and radical reversal of perspective about fortune. By the time the Buddha arrived at this understanding, he had already abandoned his riches and social position. As the story goes, he had to unshackle himself from the familial and societal binds that precluded him from seeing reality. Nobility, in the Buddhist sense, means releasing ourselves from the social constructs that blind us to the truth, positioning ourselves to receive the truth, accept the truth, and learn to live equanimously with the truth. But what is "Right" about this for African American activists engaged in anti-racism work?

Africans that were kidnapped, tortured, enslaved, and extracted from their families, neighbors, territories, countries, and continent had countless lies violently imposed on them for four hundred years. What were those lies? The lies included: Africans are not human beings; Africans are on Earth to serve Europeans; African slaves are three-fifths of a person; Africans can endure the pain and suffering of slavery; African women and men do not suffer dehumanization from being raped and abused by European men; Africans pollute Europeans; Europeans are more intelligent than Africans; and so on. There were and are countless attempts to permanently traumatize our historical and intergenerationally transmitted narratives. African American nobility, as informed by a Buddhist perspective, means releasing ourselves from the racist social constructs that blind us to the truth of our humanity, positioning ourselves to receive the truth of our humanity, accept our humanity, and learn to live equanimously with the truth of our humanity in a society that still questions it. The repetition of this sentiment is intentional. To be authentically African American aligns well with the Buddhist nobility project. Nobility, in the Buddhist sense, is synonymous with Right as it relates to the path. To be Right is to be Noble, and anti-racism activism is Noble, Right, and skillful when it counters the effects of trauma.

Understanding the Noble Eightfold Path often begins with understanding Right View. Right View is concerned with how we understand phenomena. Having experienced meditation and having grown up in the United States, a Western country that celebrates dualism (the separation of things into parts), we understand Right View can only be achieved through the mind of meditation. This meditated mind is less divided, experiences interconnection with phenomena, is not engaged in hardening ego constructions, experiences the impermanence of perspectives and frames of perception, and is not clinging to or craving anything. Right View is best supported by regular meditation practice and is supported by other Path elements, including Right Intention. When engaging in activism, having Right View can prevent polarization and delusion.

Right Intention means cultivating the mind in such a way that when negative intentions arise, we note them through mindfulness of the mind. We then use compassion meditation practices in Right Action such as lovingkindness and *tonglen* (Tibetan for "sending and receiving") to reverse the impulse to inflict harm. Clinging to negative intentions (even if we intend not to act on them) inflicts pain and suffering onto our consciousness.

Therefore, African American Buddhist practitioners work to release ourselves from negative intentions. In the US context, we must ask ourselves if we have unconsciously identified with the negative ideas, images, and associations white society has projected onto us. We must check if we harbor generational rage against white people for centuries of slavery, Jim Crow, police brutality, injustice, and mass incarceration. For our emotional well-being, we must search for authentic feelings and the sources of these feelings. For African Americans, the path offers activists a strategy for deep soul searching.

Why does our society find it necessary to imprison and disenfranchise as many African Americans as possible? Is it the case that, driven by the massive scale of unconscious white fear, white folks believe that we, the ancestors of slaves, are planning a long-overdue revolt? Is this fear projected onto us? And have some of us identified with the projection? Do we harbor *Django Unchained* fantasies when we identify with the oppression of our foreparents? Can we honor the lives of our persecuted forebearers while living equanimously with the current situation of police brutality, injustice, and mass incarceration? We can choose, with justification, to be constantly enraged, but isn't that just another form of imprisonment? Why give oppression the satisfaction of enslaving our minds to the grip of suffering? Anti-racism activists need to speak the truth of our experiences without adding to our suffering. Practicing Right Speech helps.

Right Speech is a concept we are already familiar with; we all know the power words hold to either cause harm to people or to uplift them. Some words really wound us to the core, especially those negative words that get repeatedly hurled at us from insecure, unskillful, and abusive parents or parental figures while we are individuating—the early traumas. These insults, from people who are positioned to nurture us, adhere to our evolving sense of self and become part of the self-effacing narratives that we unconsciously and consciously carry into other relationships.

Right Speech, from a Buddhist perspective, not only includes refraining from speech intended to harm oneself and others but also includes cultivating skills of speech that are nurturing, supportive, and inspiring. Right Speech, for activists, does not preclude us from criticizing unjust systems. In fact, Right Speech informs how to address injustice with the Right View of nondualism and the Right Intention of nonharming. Right Speech can help us remember that Right is Noble and the words "Right" and "Noble" also mean truthful and compassionate. Right Speech is also supported by wisdom, knowing there is a time and place for saying what needs to be said and to whom it needs to be said. Right Speech can be understood more broadly as Right Communication, which includes communicating compassionately, honestly, in a timely manner, with no intention to harm—be it through mail, email, text, social media, emojis, or body language. Therefore, we can see that Right Speech and Right Communication are different manifestations of another Path element: Right Action.

What we say, what we do, what we don't say, and what we don't do all have consequences, be they positive, negative, mixed, or neutral. Since Buddhism is the path of nonharming, it encourages the use of mindfulness to bring present-time awareness to our environment (including ourselves in our environment) and it encourages checking to see if our actions have the potential to harm or are actually harming. When we locate an impulse to cause harm, we refrain from intentionally harming by cultivating Right Intention. Furthermore, Right View helps us grow in wisdom so we can better predict how our actions might affect others and ourselves. In other words, we can't call out the harmful behaviors of others while we engage in the same harmful behaviors.

Right Action, for activists, can mean the difference between life and death. When we are confronted by a police officer, we know that virtually any movement can result in the officer shooting us dead. We've been taught to be extra careful about our actions so as not to provoke the police to act violently. We've been taught not to run, not to grab anything, to keep our empty hands in the air, not to talk back, and to do exactly as we are told—even if the experience is degrading—to save our lives. We have been taught to be extremely deferential. A spectrum and specter of trauma pervades our lives—still. Some things have not changed.

This is our heartbreaking reality, but it is not a reality we have to lose our minds and hearts over. Practicing meditation helps us to increase our awareness, slow down our aggression, hasten our empathy, and promote our creativity and civility in the midst of being threatened—even in the midst of our activism. A question Black Buddhists ponder is "What is Right Action when confronted by a violent racist?" Our actions are not just about our own self-preservation but also about the well-being of those around us, including violent perpetrators. We are concerned about how our actions lead to domino effects and we vow not to become oppressors even while being oppressed. We know that hatred does not transform hatred, only love does that. Right Action, at its core, is love. Love in Right Action applies to everything we do, including our hobbies, vocations, work, and activism. Right Action is necessary in the economic system we live in.

We live in a capitalist society. Capitalism includes not only creativity and freedom but also exploitation, poverty, classism, caste designations, racism, sexism (and other "isms" related to sex and gender), ageism, white supremacy, human supremacy, imperialism, and colonialism. It allows for shortened lifespans for poor people due to chronic stress, hunger, thirst, and treatable but untreated diseases. Conversely, capitalism allows for lengthened lifespans for poor people when wealth is shared. Right Livelihood, another path element, means not making money in a way that harms others.

How do we do this in a capitalist system and also survive as whole, spiritually integrated, nonexploitative, generous, and constructive human beings? We can begin by examining if and how greed operates in our lives. Capitalism can breed greed if we have the wrong view that possessing a multitude of things, or having much more money than we need, brings real security and real joy. Studies have shown that in the United States, being rich does not make one happy and does not promote mental, emotional, or psychological security. Having been the objects of capitalism and exploited as property, Black people through the generations, ironically, have created a collective psychological defense against the vulnerability of being seen as financially insecure. Some of us have come to value things that don't bring lasting joy. The symbols of success—a large home, a luxury car, precious gems and metals, and expensive designer clothing—and paying for these things through doing work that exploits, maims, causes addictions, or kills others, is destructive for all concerned. It feeds the delusion that being wealthy or appearing to be wealthy protects Black people from exploitation. We are not protected. Ideally, Right Livelihood promotes safety, truth, nonharming, and constructive enterprises. Right Livelihood is not the pursuit of greed and has no interest in impressing others with material excess. It is not a way to demonstrate economic viability or invulnerability. It can be used as a springboard to create economic alternatives within the system in which we find ourselves. Right Livelihood is certainly a fitting description for Right and Noble anti-racism activism, but, ironically, even that kind of work can be pursued compulsively—we can become workaholics about constructive work. Compulsive Right Livelihood is done without Right Effort, another element on the Path.

Have you ever pursued the right thing, but went about it the wrong way? Maybe you were advocating for justice while also demonizing others? Have you ever put too much energy into something only to find it took a lot less energy to produce the desired result? Have you ever thought that being nice, courteous, nonthreatening, or extremely friendly would result in white strangers not being afraid or intimidated by you, but they were anyway? If you understand that you cannot control others' perceptions and you stop trying to do so, then you are engaging in Right Effort.

A surprising thing about Right Effort is that often one only has to stop doing that habitual thing; the act of stopping, paradoxically, is the effort. What makes such an effort "Right" is the intention to do no harm. By acknowledging the reasons why we produce our own frustrations, aggravations, and burnout (because we are wired to be productive and take pride in our productivity), we choose to love ourselves and practice compassion for the habitual ways we cause our own suffering. We love ourselves even when we aren't productive. We learn to release our habits, sit with the loss, and make meaning of how we are allowing transformation to take place within our consciousness. We notice the energy arising to do what is familiar, the agitation arising when we don't know what to do next, and let it all play out with the confidence that no harm will come to anyone while this is happening. We rest.

African Americans, especially those who have been driven to succeed in our capitalist society, have lived the maxim "Be twice as good as the next white person." All in order to succeed professionally. Can we see how obsessive racism can make us? How many of us have taken this maxim to heart, impacting the health of our hearts? Heart disease, trauma, and many other ailments are rampant in our community, not because we are Black but because we have tried to survive and thrive in a racist system that has required us to work harder—like in slavery, but as free people. This is madness! Maybe the delusion that Buddhism addresses for Black people is that our collective consciousness remains enslaved. But enslaved to what, this time?

We are enslaved by habits of our unexamined minds. African Americans live the reality of racist oppression in a capitalist society wherein we compete against non-Black people for just about everything. Fortunately, for many, the competition is "friendly." There is enough food and water, but there is not enough healthy, affordable food in most neighborhoods, and the water is cleaner in some neighborhoods and more polluted in others. There is not enough affordable housing in many cities. Affordable, accessible, nonaddictive medicines are out of reach for millions of Americans. The rich and poor are pitted against one another, and it appears half of the country is ready to wage war against the other half. Our dualistic, two-party system is failing us in part because each party defines itself in opposition to the other in the quest for power. Our "news" comes from a variety of sources, whether invited or intrusive, and is available on countless channels twenty-four hours a day, every day. And so, amidst these realities of racism, competition, and constant stimulation, we become enslaved to mental habits of distraction.

What do these external, social realities distract us from? They distract us from our own internal processes. Right Mindfulness, another Path element, is the choice to bring awareness to every aspect of ourselves that we can bring our attention to. Why would we want to pay close attention to ourselves when we've grown up with so many messages telling us that we are not even worthy of others paying attention to us? The reasons are compelling, especially for activists.

We exist. Our existence is a miracle. Miracles are worthy of being witnessed. Right Mindfulness is an experience in witnessing miracles. In Right Mindfulness, we observe how our thoughts come and go, how we make meaning of this life, how we get deluded, and also how we experience freedom from delusion. We observe the body (its parts and how they function), bodily sensations, feelings, breath, and the connections between our thoughts and behavior, including speech. We can see how we become motivated to eradicate racism through a wide mixture of experiences—not just hurt and fear but also love and connection; not just rejection and isolation but also family and community; not just alienation and delusion but also awareness and self-regard. In short, it's complicated. We are a fascinating species, we are intriguing individuals, and each one of us is unique and full of mysterious surprise if we're willing to be witnesses to ourselves. To be this kind of witness, we need to make choices to not be so easily distracted by all the sensationalism and vapidity of our consumerist culture. How do we turn our attention toward ourselves?

One way to start is to begin making more discerning choices about what we take in. When we hear something that we know is gossip, we can begin renouncing any interest in the subject matter. We may have to learn how to be displeasing when we tell others we are no longer engaging in what we used to engage in, but it is more important for us to have self-knowledge than to have questionable information about people who probably have not consented to having their stories told to us. We may also annoy people who constantly come to us complaining about the same things while doing nothing to change their circumstances. Does it really help others to indulge in constant venting without sharing wisdom and skills on how to transform their suffering? When we've cleared some space for reflection and contemplation and when we've skillfully let our gossip and venting partners know we are limiting our intake to pay better attention to ourselves, then we can practice Right Mindfulness regularly. Doing so is refreshing, centering, guiding, fulfilling, and awe-inspiring. Right Mindfulness supports the other Path elements and thereby acts to decrease suffering in different ways.

On the Path to reduce our suffering, African American activists doing anti-racism work may consider the twenty-first century as our Universal Renaissance in Black Self-Knowledge. Just like the Harlem Renaissance of the 1920s was a special time for Black artists of all kinds to flourish, and just as the Black Power,

Civil Rights, and Pan-Africanist movements of the 1960s were critical causes for worldwide African liberation from imperialism and colonialism, so, too, can our twenty-first-century Black Self-Knowledge movement be a time of reclamation. Reclamation of what? Of something that seems so simple and accessible to most uncolonized people but for African Americans has been obscured by the social obstacles to full personhood that the trauma of racism has built. It is reclamation of our full humanity.

Right View, Right Intention, Right Speech, Right Action, Right Livelihood, Right Effort, and Right Mindfulness are powerful philosophies and practices that go far toward liberation from the delusion that we are not fully human, or are unworthy of respect, or are criminally minded people. However, without Right Concentration, the last Path element, the transformation is not anchored in the base of consciousness and is thus at risk of being merely cognitive, not transformative at the embodied level, and hence behaviorally superficial. What is Right Concentration?

In Right Concentration, the first stage is when the meditator practices returning their attention to the object of meditation and has some "success" keeping their mind focused on that object, with pleasant feelings accompanying the sustained focus. The second stage is marked by the cessation of attempts to bring attention to the meditation object. The effort is effortless. As effort subsides, all that is felt is happiness or joy. The third stage is the effortless cessation of happiness and the arising of equanimity. The meditator is aware of this state. The fourth stage is the end of the awareness of equanimity, though equanimity remains, effortlessly, but there is no experience of pleasure or pain. This is nondualism. There is only a scant trace of the experience of being in a body.

In short, Right Concentration is being in a deepening meditative state. For the initiate, it can be terrifying because it requires the voluntary renunciation of habituated activities, people, places, customs, and comforts while embracing meditative immersion for hours, days, weeks, months, or years at a time. Right Concentration should be approached gradually. One can start by practicing one minute of mindfulness a day, go up to several minutes a day, then to twenty to thirty minutes a day. Some people go on to an hour a day, three to four hours during a weekend, to the whole weekend, a week, and so on.

It is helpful when experiments in Right Concentration are supported by experienced meditation teachers and students and are hosted in places that have a long history of hosting meditation retreats. One way to assess whether a meditation retreat center is right for you is to check if their retreat applications or other introductory processes ask about the applicant's meditation experiences and the applicant's former and present meditation teachers and communities. This application process helps the retreat center know if and how they can support the applicant and it helps the applicant know whether the retreat center is in the position to support them during this emotionally and mentally vulnerable time. Long meditation retreats evoke mental and emotional vulnerability because returning to one's object of meditation over and over again can trigger traumas, known and unknown. In addition, mindfulness teachings should not be brought to people in psychotic states because such teachings are likely to exacerbate the psychosis. The same can occur with deep states of meditation. Not knowing our traumas and those that arise in activism or not knowing how our traumas are impacted by meditation, however, should not be taken to mean that meditation is not right. The real questions are these: What type of meditation retreat is appropriate? How long? How often? To what end?

Why would an African American anti-racism activist want to experience Right Concentration? If we were willing to momentarily experience ourselves without traumatized history—without the constructs of race, ethnicity, gender, and religion and without preferences and desires, fears and terrors, anger and rage— imagine how much freedom there may be. We would come out of that experience knowing ourselves as part of the Universal Renaissance in Black Self-Knowledge that has collectively escaped us because it didn't serve white capitalist interests for us to know ourselves as connected to the universe. Put another way, Right

Concentration may heal our wounded self-perception as being disconnected, segregated, Jim Crowed, and imprisoned. It may return us to the African notion of *ntu*—knowing ourselves as connected to all that is.

"Trauma" is a term used in this introduction and frequently appears in the essays in this volume. So, what is trauma, really, and why do we focus on it?

WHAT'S TRAUMA GOT TO DO WITH IT?

There are many definitions for trauma, but one that stands out comes from Dr. Bessel van der Kolk. The author of *The Body Keeps Score: Brain, Mind, and Body in the Healing of Trauma*, van der Kolk is a pioneering researcher in the field of trauma studies and has redefined the scope of trauma. He writes, "Trauma is not just an event that took place sometime in the past; it is also the imprint left by that experience on mind, brain, and body. This imprint has ongoing consequences for how the human manages to survive."[1] We (the editors of this volume) are clinicians, professors of pastoral and spiritual care, and Buddhist practitioners interested in how Buddhist practices help people manage their survival in a cultural context that won't let up. We believe that persistent practice cultivates resiliency.

Because of our experiences in living a Buddhist lifestyle (which does not require one to be religious or even a Buddhist) and knowing other African-descended Buddhist practitioners, and the research I (Yetunde) did with African-descended lesbians in the Insight Meditation community,[2] we have faith that practitioner-activists can manage their traumas, past and present. Based on this belief, we encourage ourselves and our clients, students, and fellow activists to dispense with the pretense of having to appear as if we have everything under control. Why? Right View reminds us of the truth: we all are vulnerable to trauma at any time.

Trauma can be present in our day-to-day lives. The deaths of loved ones, job losses, divorces, and public disasters can all be experienced as traumatic. Trauma can also happen from an event in the past; sexual abuses, illnesses, and losses of close relatives can contribute to the trauma-induced cognitive imprint that impairs our functioning. And, as if our personal existences were not complicated enough, as Black folks, we can be traumatically affected by the experience of historical racism. We call this the trauma of being Black in the United States.

Being traumatized influences the way we react to the ordinary and unusual challenges in our lives. When we experience something unpleasant or uninvited, we can become angry, frustrated, and scared. We may worry about how to handle any number of situations. We might blame others for our mistakes. Many of us struggle with constant anxiety, which affects sleep and memory, causes high blood pressure, and can depress our mood and lead to troubling behaviors. When we experience something unpleasant or uninvited, we are often actually responding to the memory of old traumas. But our response to the situation or circumstance at hand can be inappropriate, leaving us and others confused. Coupling van der Kolk's definition of trauma with a Buddhist understanding of what it means to be human, we arrive at the proposition that when we are not effectively managing the traumas we experience, we are suffering. Right Action includes self-care. The most obvious manifestation of the trauma of being alive is evident in the high levels of anxiety we see everywhere in society: homes, schools, colleges, workplaces, hospitals, traffic, buses, grocery stores, and coffee shops. Everywhere people gather where they are not managing the imprint of trauma, we see anxiety and consequent difficulty in managing our survival.

As professors at Harvard Divinity School and United Theological Seminary (Giles and Yetunde, respectively), and as a teacher in Upaya Zen Center's Buddhist Chaplaincy training program (Yetunde), we teach courses about trauma, spiritual care, compassionate care of the dying, interreligious spiritual care, cultural competency in spiritual care, couples counseling, and Buddhist spiritual care. The students we teach are talented, highly motivated, and passionate about creating a world where compassion, justice, and respect for others is the foundation of a healthy society. Our spiritual care students are activists in their own right. Many of them are seekers who experience the trauma of being alive when the beliefs, values, and practices they hold collide with the white privilege they navigate in an anxious world. For some, these classes are their first experiences of being in a multireligious space, and part of their work is to integrate those diverse parts so they do not bring fractured selves to the people and communities they are called to care for. Our students strive to use their gifts to heal the world and support communities of meaning where they find purpose and hope. For Black students whose existential anxiety is largely because of racism in their lives, their culturally induced anxiety is a stark reminder that trauma is persistent and deep, linking them to the experience of racism from slavery to the present. Though trauma is persistent and deep, we believe trauma is workable and transmutable, and Buddhist practices (secularized or otherwise) can effectively contribute to the transmutation.

Dr. Joy DeGruy, the author of the groundbreaking book *Post Traumatic Slave Syndrome*, traces the history of Black trauma in America and how this trauma has been passed down from generation to generation. DeGruy believes Black people inherit intergenerational trauma and thus experience anxiety in every facet of their daily lives. The trauma of being alive while Black is not new. The trauma of being alive is not limited to race, class, location, sexual orientation, gender, religion, or political party. We all suffer from some form of cognitive imprints that leave us unable to see reality for what it is, and our resistance to understanding and accepting the trauma of being alive keeps us endlessly running like caged hamsters on a wheel. In Buddhism, we call this *samsara*—the endless cycle of suffering. From the perspective of Right Effort, running like hamsters in a wheel in a cage doesn't produce enlightenment, just samsara. What are we to do to get off the wheel and out of the cage?

More than twenty-five hundred years ago, the Buddha offered us a way off the wheel and out of the cage, breaking the samsaric cycle toward enlightenment. How? We return to the Four Noble Truths and the Noble Eightfold Path. In the First Noble Truth, we are reminded that no matter what we do to avoid suffering, life involves suffering. There is no escaping illness, aging, and death, though there are a multitude of ways we foolishly and contrarily try to experience perpetual health, youthfulness, and everlasting life. All of us suffer, and there is no shame in that.

According to Buddhist lore, the Buddha began to suffer when he was Siddhartha Gautama, the prince who had not yet left his home and place of privilege. After years of living in a community gated from everyday people, in a moment of differentiation from his father, he unexpectedly confronted the reality of illness, aging, and death when he saw others outside the gate. By witnessing the traumas of other people being alive, he saw himself as just like them. Was it shocking for him? Yes. Traumatizing? For sure. Gautama's trauma disoriented him and triggered a spiritual crisis in his own life. His life-altering experience led him away from wealth into the poverty of the forest to reflect on how to end suffering, which became the foundational experiences for developing the Four Noble Truths.

The Truths and the path may well be antidotes to treating the trauma of being alive today as we face greater challenges in caring and activism in the world. However, those of us who are activists, caregivers, or work in professions that demand presence and compassion for the suffering of others may find ourselves burdened by attending to the trauma of others. The cost of caring is high for caregivers. The terms "vicarious trauma" or "secondary trauma" refer to the emotional residue that caregivers experience when they listen to people's stories and they bear witness to the pain, fear, and terror of others. This exposure to the trauma of others may negatively affect the caregivers, but again, there is no shame in any of this. If the suffering of trauma is our shared reality, how do we best live in this reality with resilience?

In her book *Trauma Stewardship: An Everyday Guide to Caring for Self While Caring for Others*, Laura van Dernoot Lipsky developed a model of caring for caregivers to remain effective and avoid the negative effects of caring for others. She identified the consequences of trauma exposure for caregivers as follows: an inability to empathize, addiction, an inflated sense of the importance of one's work, feeling helpless or hopeless, a sense that one can never do enough, hypervigilance, diminished creativity, an inability to embrace complexity, minimizing the painful and debilitating effects of chronic exhaustion or physical ailments, an inability to listen or deliberate avoidance, dissociative moments, and a sense of persecution, guilt, fear, anger, or cynicism.

We have also seen the consequences of trauma exposure in African American anti-racism activists. How can resiliency be cultivated in this toxic mixture? Van Dernoot Lipsky designed the Five Directions, a navigational tool that engages caregivers in various contexts in building our capacity for trauma stewardship. Each direction provides space for reflection about our intentions and is consistent with the Noble Eightfold Path.[3]

Creating Space for Inquiry: focusing on the present and understanding our intention. "How do I come to this work?" Remind yourself that you are making a choice. Consider whether this choice is in the best interest of serving others. This is Right Intention.

Choosing Our Focus: shifting our perspective to rediscover our inspiration and passion. "How am I affected by it?" Think of a challenging work situation. Commit to one day of paying attention to the thoughts that flow through your mind. Notice whether those thoughts are positive, loving, or kind. This is Right Mindfulness.

Building Compassion and Community: creating and connecting to an environment that sustains us. "How do I make sense of and learn from my experience?" Ask yourself how your ancestors or benefactors found healing. Will some of their practices be useful for you? Reflect on the unconditional love you receive from your ancestors or benefactors. This is Right View.

Finding Balance: achieving balance and moving energy through reconnecting to inner strength, honoring, change, and impermanence. "How do I manage my trauma exposure?"

Commit to using deep breathing to ground yourself. Write a daily gratitude page in a journal. This is Right Mindfulness and Right Concentration.

Daily Practice of Centering Ourselves: shifting our practice of caregiving over time. "What can I put down?" Set an intention for the day. Arguably, being centered daily is the whole of the Buddhist practice.

Van Dernoot Lipsky's model of trauma stewardship, like other Western psychological models of care, expand on the ancient cognitive behavioral model of the Noble Eightfold Path. Within trauma stewardship we find notions of Right Intention, Right Mindfulness, Right View, and Right Concentration, but in our modern and postmodern consciousnesses, we know we can't use the word "suffering" to describe the varieties of our suffering. In other words, trauma is suffering and more than suffering. However, the heart of this schema relies heavily on the daily practice of centering oneself. Activists and caregivers need a rigorous and consistent practice to create self-compassion, openness, equanimity, and resiliency. Secular or religious Buddhism, as a set of ethics or psychology and as a way of life or a philosophy, goes a long way toward making being alive *livable*.

We live in a culture that finds the trauma of being alive challenging. Television and social media provide ways to live in a fantasy with endless promises of beauty, success, money, health, power, food, and clothing. Nothing short of paradise. We cannot carry the immense pain of suffering alone; attempting to do so exacerbates the pain and suffering by covering it with isolation and alienation. The First Noble Truth invites us to welcome our wounds and meet our suffering with courage and compassion. To hold space for someone else who is suffering—while replacing fear and judgment with acceptance of the trauma of being alive—is a radical act of standing in awe. But we must commit ourselves to living lives of resiliency. How?

Several years ago, I (Yetunde) began researching the psychospiritual lives of African American Buddhist lesbians in the Insight Meditation community. Insight Meditation comes out of the Theravada Buddhist tradition. In the Insight Meditation community, one learns how to practice mindfulness and Vipassana meditation, is encouraged to participate in meditation retreats, and learns about the concept of "no self." In brief, mindfulness is nonjudgmental awareness of one's body, feelings, breath, and thoughts. In Vipassana meditation, the meditator focuses on an object of meditation that the meditator returns to repeatedly for long periods of time. No self (a concept with many definitions, some contradictory and controversial) means interdependency. It also means "no soul" according to how the ancient Vedic traditions understood the connection between certain human beings and their creator-God. No self is a complicated concept that is concerned with negation, boundarylessness, egolessness, and castelessness. Based on our clinical and personal Buddhist practice experiences, we'd like to think that no self does not mean no animating energy within the body. In other words, we believe energy is embodied. Through our work, we have seen how energy can shift from depression to elation to calm. For the purposes of this chapter, we will call that animating energy "soul," and we believe African American anti-racism activism, spiritual care, and Buddhist practice are soul work. Soul is grounded, paradoxically boundless, and makes resiliency possible.

The soul that is grounded has a mixture of imagination for a better world, ethical commitments to the well-being of one's self and others, courage, and a willingness to experience unpleasant sensations (trauma) in one's body to bring about a new world. This grounded soul is in the body and is the body. The soul that is boundless is that same mixture and is also a permeable, transmuting, infinitesimal, and vulnerable particle in the cosmos. What does this grounded and paradoxically boundless soul have to do with resiliency and sustaining soulfulness for activism and caregiving?

According to the research referenced in this chapter, mindfulness, meditation, and no self, as interdependent concepts, contribute to resiliency in our relationships—*even with people unlike ourselves*. And it is *not* dependent upon whether they like us. To manifest our visions of a new world, a world that is and will be inhabited by people we don't know, we don't like, and may not like us, we have to be in some level of relationship with them, and them with us. How can we do that in such a way that we experience resiliency while others benefit? As you contemplate being in relationship with people you do not like and don't like you, notice if there is any tension in your body. Breathe in and breathe out three times, noticing when you are breathing in and when you are breathing out. This is the simple practice of being mindful of the breath. You need not be a Buddhist to commit to living a nonanxious lifestyle. Relaxing enhances relational resiliency because it does not transmit the energy of anxiety onto those around you.

If mindfulness of the breath feels right for you and you practice it daily for a while, it will be time for you to consider a half-day mindfulness meditation retreat. Learning how to be mindful (including mindful sitting and walking) for hours at a time can cultivate a wholesome desire for a lifestyle conducive to inspiring peace in others. How? We have found that people are better able to be with people who are peaceful than those who are anxious. That probably comes as no surprise. A peaceful countenance nonverbally invites others to be themselves and in being one's self in the presence of another, one learns who they are without the threat of being judged. It is here you might ask, "How can I be myself when you say there is no Self?"

The definition of No Self, for purposes of this chapter, means soul and interdependence. We did not come into being by our own volition, we do not exist by our own volition, nor do we go out of existence by our own volition. In the cosmos, we are permeable, transmuting infinitesimal, and vulnerable particles, and when we understand ourselves as such, we can begin to release delusions about each one of us being rugged, self-reliant individuals able to change the world all by ourselves. Our grounded soul is grounded in a connected collective—and that is what makes it boundless. Groundedness and boundlessness are known and felt through meditation; meditation becomes a lifestyle. Meditation as a lifestyle contributes to remarkable relational resilience, and remarkable relational resilience is another expression of soul sustenance. Sound too good to be true?

Paradoxically, African American anti-racism activists who are in the fight for our lives, our dignity, and our world will have to stop fighting—for moments at a time, sometimes even for long moments. We will have to trust that when we are not fighting, someone else is. We don't always know who the warriors are, what their tactics are, or how long they will fight, but we do know that if we don't cultivate peace of mind in the midst of external strife, we will do the opponent's job for them. Nothing is better for the opponent than our own self destruction. Why give them that satisfaction? Informed by black feminist lesbian poet Audre Lorde, we believe the act of self-preservation in the face of another's attempt to annihilate us is one of the highest forms of spiritual practice there is. Mindfulness, meditation, and no self is self-preservation and contributes to remarkable relational resilience. Let us commit to cultivating peace of mind and peace of body as we struggle for liberation. Let us be refuges for each other so that our collective souls and collective selves may be nourished for generations of communities to come, and let our rest be used for the reparative work we know is ahead of us.

There is a trauma of being alive and there is a trauma of being alive while Black. These traumas, when unmanaged, get tangled with the traumas in society and within the people we advocate and care for. Past unmanaged traumas leave imprints and distort Right View, leaving us and others confused about why we say and do what we do when what we say and what we do doesn't match the situation at hand. The Buddha is not known to have developed an understanding of trauma with the same vocabulary we speak of trauma today, but even as far back as twenty-five hundred years ago, the understanding that not possessing Right View, Right Mindfulness, Right Intention, Right Livelihood, Right Concentration, Right Action, Right Speech, and Right Effort meant that the imprints and consequences for managing our survival remained. Are we doing a good job of managing our imprints? Are we living Nobly and Rightly?

Our country and world have experienced a rise in nationalism, and within the understanding of each nation's nationalism, each nation has a heightened focus on who it believes belongs and who does not. Scores of people are being deported, visas are being denied in greater numbers, entry restrictions on non-European countries are on the rise, and Islamophobia informs immigration policies, all impacting the white- to non-white ratio of people in the United States.

In fact, one potentially traumatizing slogan that has been used in the United States against African Americans is "Go back to Africa where you belong!" Black belonging has always been contested in the United States and we are now being asked to support the exclusion of Brown people at our borders, Black people from African countries, and the Muslim world which is largely populated by people of color. For what? The promise of employment— but not the promise of employment that will pay for the rapidly rising cost of housing in our cities, the cost of private schools as public schools remain under attack, or the exorbitantly rising cost of college.

What is happening to us when we give voice or support to anti-immigrant messages like "We don't want you here"? How do these messages trigger past traumas and create new ones? If this is the time of the Universal Renaissance in Black Self-Knowledge, it is also the time of our universal responsibility— the work of Black Buddhism and its bodhisattvas, those who put the liberation of others before their own liberation.

In *Black and Buddhist: What Buddhism Can Teach Us About Race, Resilience, Transformation, and Freedom*, African American Buddhist leaders and scholars Gyōzan Royce Andrew Johnson, Cheryl A. Giles, Ruth King, Kamilah Majied, Lama Rod Owens, Lama Dawa Tarchin Phillips, Sebene Selassie, and Pamela Ayo Yetunde offer their unique perspectives on what it has meant for us to survive and thrive while being Black in our families, communities, and in the United States. These contributors have been formed in a variety of Buddhist traditions including Community of Mindful

Living, Insight Meditation, Shambhala, Soka Gakkai, Soto Zen, and Tibetan—and often in more than one Buddhist tradition. Each contributor is also a gendered being, each differing in gender and sexual expressions. Collectively, our offerings are informed by Catholic, Christian, Hindu, and Muslim traditions, as well as immigrant (African and European) and native-born perspectives. Our perspectives are mixed with Western and Buddhist psychologies. We also offer what has been learned by living as Black-white biracial persons. Buddhist wisdom and practices have been integrated into our complex subjectivities, defying the notion that Blackness and being Buddhist are monolithic. You may find a part of yourself in our stories, but our hope is that you will find your story and be true to that.

On the dedication page in the front matter of this book, we list early African American Buddhist teachers who helped pave the way for the Buddhist-informed Universal Renaissance in Black Self-Knowledge we are in. There is a common Buddhist practice called dedicating the merit whereby we commit the fruits of our spiritual practices to the well-being of others. In like fashion, we dedicate *Black and Buddhist* to you.

· 1 ·

THEY SAY THE PEOPLE COULD FLY

Disrupting the Legacy of Sexual Violence
through Myth, Memory, and Connection

CHERYL A. GILES

> There was a great outcryin. The bent backs straightened
> up. Old and young who were called slaves and could fly
> joined hands. . . . Say they flew away to *Free-dom*.[1]
> —VIRGINIA HAMILTON, *The People Could Fly: American Black Folktale*

> The real story is that the people who were
> treated like beasts did not become beastly.[2]
> —TONI MORRISON, "Toni Morrison Among Us"

THE YEAR 2019 marked the four hundredth anniversary of
American slavery. It was in 1619 when the first slavers' boat arrived
on the shores of Virginia, where shackled West Africans were sold
to colonists. Most of us know little about the history of slavery
and how it spurred the development of capitalism in the United
States. The seeds of economic growth were sowed by enslaved African men and women, whose brutalized bodies were traumatized
under a system of white supremacy that generated wealth and

solidified power. Slavery remains a painful period in American history, both contested and sanitized to help us digest the horrific tragedy and loss of millions of enslaved black bodies who died in servitude and remain unknown. The four hundredth anniversary arrived at a time when persistent anti-black and anti-immigrant violence had reached epidemic proportions. The legacy of black enslaved bodies is a powerful example of the enduring spirit of resistance and love that serves as a reminder that freedom is possible.

This chapter is a reflection on bearing witness to the impact of intergenerational trauma on the body. With the support of mentors, I found the courage to use my pain as a pathway to healing, which enabled me to help others. As a clinical psychologist working with traumatized black adolescents and their families, I found that moments of awakening often occurred for me as passing flashes of recognition of my connection with these families. These moments quickly evaporated from my consciousness but embedded themselves within my body; I remember feeling a tightness in my throat that rendered me speechless as I witnessed their suffering. Interacting with these families, observing the pervasive trauma in their lives, pushed me to seek psychotherapy. I didn't yet understand that the affinity I felt with these families was linked to my own history of intergenerational trauma.

For many years, I hid behind an imaginary armor of control, believing I could will myself through any experience. I believed I was keeping my trauma experience contained. Slowly, however, I was becoming unhinged; I began to fear that my clients and coworkers could sense my fragility. I was losing control and needed help. I found a therapist who saw me as I was: queer, black, Buddhist, and searching for relief from suffering; I found a therapist who was not afraid to walk this journey with me. I started going to therapy every week to attempt to understand how and why my mind and body would automatically go into overdrive when I was triggered by unresolved trauma. Despite trying to look normal, I felt a growing unease with the thoughts, feelings, and sensations I was holding inside. Deep down, generations of trauma were rumbling through me, wanting to be free. Part of me was terrified to release the swell of so much pain, and another part wanted to hide from the chaos.

Educating ourselves about trauma and learning to be present to feelings, thoughts, and sensations require new skills to ground ourselves and find safety in the body. Similar to therapy, meditation can help us develop awareness, sit with uncertainty, be present to our own discomfort, and learn to befriend ourselves. My experiences learning about the impact of traumatic response in the body are threaded through this chapter. Examples of meditation practices that have been useful to me are included at the end.

MYTH: REMEMBERING ENSLAVED BLACK BODIES

Stories of resistance, transcendence, and collective liberation are deeply embedded in African American oral tradition. The survival of these stories enables closer examination of enslaved men and women's reactions to the horrific violence slaveholders unleashed upon them. These stories, and others like them, make for excruciatingly painful but necessary reading. Understanding the meaning of freedom requires grappling with the "dangerous memory of slavery,"[3] where black bodies were destroyed. Recalling torture, lynching, and sexual violence is indeed both powerful and dangerous, and remembering is necessary for uncovering and claiming the loss of millions of enslaved black men and women, people who were despised and treated as inhuman, people who never became "beastly."

Myths and folklore are tools of healing and resistance. For example, "The Myth of the Flying Africans," which refers to events dating back to 1803, was passed down from generation to generation.[4] It was a narrative of West African Ibo people, who were captured and transported in overcrowded and squalid conditions across the Atlantic by cargo ship to the coasts of Georgia and South Carolina to be sold as slaves. According to the legend, when the ship landed and the Ibos realized they were being sold into slavery, they rose up, broke out of their chains, and abandoned the ship. Walking along the coastline, they began singing and chanting. By exercising their moral agency, the Ibos demonstrated resourcefulness—they were not victims to be pitied. Resisting confinement, they refused to stop dreaming of what was possible for them beyond slavery.

Refusing to be sold, some drowned themselves to avoid capture—others took flight back to Africa. Indeed, in some oral accounts, the Ibos grew wings and soared above their confinement, daring to embrace freedom and refusing to surrender. The renowned children's book author Virginia Hamilton offers a different rendering of this narrative, calling it "The People Could Fly."[5] Hamilton's version opens with the following preamble:

> They say the people could fly. Say that long ago in Africa, some of the people knew magic. And they would walk up on the air like climbin up on a gate. And they flew like blackbirds over the fields. Black, shiny wings flappin against the blue up there.
>
> Then, many of the people were captured for Slavery. The ones that could fly shed their wings. They couldn't take their wings across the water on the slave ships. Too crowded, don't you know.
>
> The folks were full of misery, then. Got sick with the up and down of the sea. So they forgot about flyin when they could no longer breathe the sweet scent of Africa.
>
> Say the people who could fly kept their power, although they shed their wings. . . .

They worked along with other folks in the field. All the workers heard the sting of the overseer's words. They all felt the snarl of the driver's whip around their legs. They all felt their clothes being torn to rags and their legs bleeding onto the earth.

But one of the slaves remembered "the ancient words that were a dark promise," the words that would allow the slaves to fly again. Seeing one after another of his people falling from the heat and the brutal forced labor, he raised his arms out to them and cried out, "*Kum kunka yali, kum . . . tambe!*"

There was a great outcryin. The bent backs straightened up. Old and young who were called slaves and could fly joined hands. Say like they would ring-sing. . . . They rose on air. They flew in a flock that was black against the heavenly blue. Black crows or black shadows. It didn't matter, they went so high. Way above the plantation, way over the slavery land. Say they flew away to *Free-dom*.

In Hamilton's version of the tale, the Africans left their wings in their homeland when they were transported to America and enslaved. Brutalized by violence, the Ibos called upon their endowed power to fly away to freedom. Because of their deeply held faith, they believed the loss of freedom was more catastrophic than dying. With freedom came the awakening that the end of suffering was possible. Drawing upon the metaphor of flight as a tool for liberation, "The People Could Fly" and other folktales demonstrate the resilience of slaves in finding freedom and safety for themselves and others.

MEMORY: CONFRONTING SEXUAL VIOLENCE AND TRAUMA

> . . . when we speak we are afraid
> our words will not be heard
> nor welcomed
> but when we are silent
> we are still afraid
>
> So it is better to speak
> remembering
> we were never meant to survive.[6]
> —AUDRE LORDE, "A Litany for Survival"

Remembering is necessary. This truth applies to recalling the tragedies of slavery, just as it applies to protecting the myths and folktales created by enslaved people, thereby marking how elements of the past reverberate still today.

This is my truth: As a thirteen-year-old in the 1930s, my mother was sexually abused by a family friend and became pregnant. The perpetrator was not held accountable. As a result of this violence, my mother's mind and body were affected in ways that defined the rest of our lives.

My maternal grandmother was a poor, black, single mother with three young children; she was ill-equipped to take care of her own kids, let alone an unwanted grandchild. All I know about her is this: she was likely a former slave, descended from a group of Gullah people of South Carolina who migrated north and settled in Hartford, Connecticut, where there was a growing community of black people. My mother gave birth to her baby and was sent to a state-run vocational school while the baby was sent to an orphanage. Terrified, ashamed, and heartbroken over leaving her mother and newborn baby, my mother withdrew into the only safety she knew: herself. She never fully recovered. Years later, she married my father and was reunited with her baby, my sister. They settled in New Haven, Connecticut, close to my father's proud, large family, and hoped to start their own family.

My mother's happiness was short-lived. Her tragic experience left her a fearful and anxious woman; she struggled with depression for the rest of her life. She did have periods of thriving. She was an accomplished cook, outgoing and funny, and she loved to dance. But she gradually lost her sparkle, a sparkle extinguished by the trauma that lived within her. Gone were the moments of lightheartedness and joy. Her energy seemed to leak out of her body until there was no joy left. Without having the resources necessary for healing, my mother suffered greatly trying to live in her own skin. There was nowhere to hide. Living with the triple whammy of being black, abused, and depressed, she was achingly alone. Family members witnessed the crumbling of her spirit, but wouldn't or couldn't help. Perhaps it was fear or ignorance or shame that blinded them to her pain. Mental illness was and remains a taboo in our culture. Post-traumatic stress disorder had not yet been identified and described, and treatment for survivors of sexual violence was not available. As business owners (a rarity in the black community of New Haven), my uncles and their families kept their distance from my mother. They were well-known in their social and business circles and feared becoming outcasts and the subjects of gossiping tongues.

We all yearn for love, connection, and belonging. This is our birthright: we are all endowed with original goodness and the capacity to love ourselves and one another. But many of us feel unworthy of this birthright. Trauma has the power to disrupt our ability to love wholeheartedly by triggering painful memories of harm in our minds, bodies, and spirits, and this creates a barrier to connection. My mother's trauma affected her ability to raise her young daughter (my sister) and she often unleashed unwarranted anger and harshness upon her own child. Sadly, my mother's trauma-related behavior resulted in my sister's suffering and her own unmet need for love and belonging.

Unlike my mother, who had no support, my sister found refuge in our paternal grandmother, who sheltered her from my mother's anger and provided love and nurturing. With our grandmother's help and by being surrounded by playful cousins and family activities, my sister learned to navigate my mother's erratic moods and anger. My sister was a motivated student and after graduating from high school, she attended nursing school with the goal of working at a local hospital in New Haven. Years after my mother died, I found boxes of old family photos with pictures of my sister at fifteen, smiling while she rode her bike with her dog, Trixie, who sat in the straw basket attached to the handlebars. These pictures offer glimpses of her occasional happiness.

My father worked as a construction laborer doing seasonal work while my mother cleaned houses for wealthy Jewish families in a suburb of New Haven. During the winter months, he collected unemployment. With the money they earned, they managed to cobble together enough to buy a house in a neighborhood within walking distance of downtown New Haven, where white flight was creeping across the city.

While trying to have another child, my mother experienced several miscarriages. After giving up on having more children, she became pregnant and gave birth to me in 1954, almost nineteen years after my sister was born. It was quite a surprise to both of my parents, and not necessarily a happy one. My father nearly forty years old and my mother, though just in her mid-thirties, having already been a parent for twenty years, they bore the scars of a hard life.

Right before my arrival, my mother had been ambivalent about parenting again. After I was born, however, she began to show signs of deep distress. Perhaps it was postpartum depression. More likely, she was triggered by memories of sexual abuse. Her sadness was exacerbated by loneliness; my father worked long hours at grimy construction sites.

My father was a talented carpenter who built wood furniture in his spare time. After applying to join the carpenters' union and being rejected several times, he learned that the union was all-white and did not accept black people. Knowing that he was excluded based purely on the color of his skin and not his skills became a tipping point for my father. Wounded by the not-so-subtle daily microaggressions at work, his anger simmered. The more he struggled to make a decent wage, the deeper his resentment grew. His shame was overwhelming. As the oldest of six children, with three brothers who were successfully self-employed, he felt the weight of failure. He was the man of the family, and he was consumed by the lack of opportunities to succeed in this role. Often, when he arrived at home, tired and angry, he repeated the same mantra to me: "Stay in school and get an education and don't get pregnant." In my nine-year-old mind, my father's words only emphasized the importance of education. What I couldn't comprehend was his warning that sex, consensual or otherwise, could upend my education. If I got pregnant, no matter the circumstances, it would be my fault. I had no idea what he meant when he talked about sex or getting pregnant, but I took his warning to mean I would be punished, and that was enough to let me know there was no room for mistakes.

Years later, I remember watching the evening news with my parents as Martin Luther King Jr. marched in Memphis, boycotting the poor conditions of sanitation workers and the union's refusal to recognize black workers. Not only was my father struggling to find happiness in his marriage to my mother but he was also facing unfair impediments to finding work that would enable him to support his family. Owning a home was a source of pride, but there were other dreams he held in his heart that went unfulfilled. His preoccupation with fulfilling his role as head of the house and getting ahead blinded him to the emotional avalanche that was building inside my mother. He was unable to see the storm that engulfed her and attend to her desperate need for love, attention, and connection. Looking back, it's difficult to imagine that she had the emotional resources to nurture a baby. Despite that, I know she loved me fiercely and protected me. I was still a young child when my sister was working her way through nursing school and was engaged to be married.

When I was nearly five years old and about to start kindergarten, my mother was hospitalized for the first time. She was totally worn out. No one saw this coming, which is still hard for me to imagine. In her misery, my mother was overwhelmed with worry that someone was going to hurt her. Her mind was racing, stalked by her internal demons. She became wildly tearful and uncontrollable, perhaps driven by a flashback to the sexual violence she longed to forget.

I remember seeing her, one day, panicking with an irrational urgency to run from the house while my father was at work. What followed was the first of three hospitalizations my mother endured from that early trauma. The American Psychological Association defines trauma as "an emotional response to a terrible event like an accident, rape, or natural disaster. Immediately after the event, shock and denial are typical. Longer term reactions include unpredictable emotions, flashbacks, strained relationships, and even physical symptoms like headaches and nausea."[7] Trauma is not a single story—each person experiences and manages it in their own unique way.

During the time my mother was hospitalized, my father cared for me with the help of my sister and other relatives. The invisible but enduring stress embedded in my mother's body was the consequential damage caused by trauma. She had no language to communicate this unbearable violation. How does a person recover from sexual violence? The shame is overwhelming. There is no one to say, "It's not your fault," "I'm sorry he hurt you," or "This should never have happened to you." Without the support of family, community, and good mental health care, my mother was never able to face her trauma and find healing. Now, I can say this: I was never afraid my mother would harm me when she was unraveling. My greatest sadness is that, when she desperately needed help, no one was there to support her. She was caught in a powerful, destructive web of violence, part of the historical legacy of seeing black bodies, especially black women's bodies, as expendable.

Despite having these traumatic experiences and the uncertainty of her mental health, my mother was able to show her love for me. She rebounded after the third hospitalization and focused her attention on caring for me. Although she left the hospital with medication, she refused to take it, complaining it made her feel dull and sleepy. Buoyed by her release from the hospital and renewed vigor from focusing on my welfare, she guided me all the way through high school, accepting help from the nuns who taught me. When I faced challenges understanding math, she became my tutor and worked tirelessly until I understood the material. Our home came alive. My mother planted flower and vegetable gardens and shared them with neighbors. She spent time cooking creative meals and repainting the rooms inside our home. It was as if my progress gave her a sense of hope, and she focused that hope on cultivating beauty all around us.

My mother's ability to connect with friends and family was renewed—with the exception of my father, whom she showed no warmth. It was as if my mother recognized that the bright flame of love and passion she once felt for my father was now a dim flicker of light. Whatever reconciliation that needed to take place was beyond my scope of understanding. Something had radically shifted for her. Although they appeared as a couple for family gatherings and on holidays, and though at home my mother played the role of dutiful wife—cleaning the house, paying bills, and washing clothes—an imaginary line was drawn between my parents, and my father accepted this boundary. He helped where he could with grocery shopping and making repairs in the house. There was no meanness, but their lack of intimacy was not lost on me.

When it came to me, however, my parents worked together and were joined in their decisions about my education. Growing up, I learned to accept their relationship and felt confident that I would be cared for, regardless of how they were with each other. Above all, my parents worked hard to help me to rise above the pain and suffering they experienced. Their aspiration was assuring I had access to a good education, and they were prepared to block any interference. Their instructions were clear: if you abide by what we are asking of you, and if you do the necessary work, success will follow. When I achieved each goal, from high school graduation to getting a doctoral degree, they breathed a sigh of relief. Though they had little, allowing me to stand on their shoulders to climb higher brought them deep gratitude and personal freedom.

CONNECTION: #METOO

In the history of the United States, the trauma to black women's enslaved bodies—bodies viewed as property, treated as objects of toil, reproduction, and pleasure—is widespread and institutionalized. These bodies have survived centuries of domination under white supremacy. With no legal protection, black women's bodies are easy prey, easy to both dehumanize and hypersexualize. For all women, but for black women especially, the recent emergence of the #MeToo movement is a wake-up call signaling that body terrorism upholds the false belief that some bodies are more valuable than others.[8]

Long before #MeToo, my mother was one of those girls who was devalued, physically and spiritually. I can only imagine how the presence of the #MeToo movement could have affected my mother. What if she had been able to come forward and find support and resources for healing? Connecting with others and knowing she was not alone might have provided a lifeline and given her hope. These resources did not exist for my mother at a time when a victim of sexual violence generally had no voice. Often, if a girl gave birth to a baby born out of wedlock, her family helped to care for the baby. Shrouded in silence and secrecy, that girl and her family bore the burden of stigmatization, loss of respect, and invisibility. And so it was for my mother.

Tarana Burke, the founder of the #MeToo movement, offers another perspective on the kind of trauma suffered by my mother and countless other black women. Growing up in the Bronx, Burke was sexually abused as a child and assaulted as a teenager. Fortunately, her mother helped her through her horrific experiences and supported her recovery, encouraging her to read inspirational books by Audre Lorde, Toni Morrison, and Alex Haley. Her mother's skillful counsel protected Burke from feeling alone, isolated, and unworthy. Burke acknowledges that, with her mother's encouragement, instead of withdrawing from social engagement, she connected with other young girls of color in her community. Maintaining a link with others and avoiding isolation helped Burke begin the long process of healing and becoming an advocate for young girls in communities of color. In 2003, unwilling to accept the ritual of abuse as inevitable, Tarana Burke founded an organization to support these young girls.

For more than two decades, Burke has advocated tirelessly for racial justice and against sexual violence, disrupting the culture of silence and invisibility that exists for traumatized girls of color. After finishing college, Burke began a career as a Civil Rights activist and youth worker in Selma, Alabama, facilitating culturally informed workshops in a junior high school. Burke founded Just Be, a nonprofit that provides access to resources, safe spaces, and empowerment for young girls in low-income communities of color. As a youth worker, she listened to girls who often came from troubled homes and had suffered in silence, afraid to share their stories of abuse and neglect.

In one heartbreaking story, Burke recalls a young girl who confided that she was being sexually abused by her mother's boyfriend. As she considered how to care for this young girl and so many others struggling with depression, behavioral problems, and difficulty learning in school, however, Burke's own experience of sexual violence began to haunt her once again. Overwhelmed and faced with her own truth, Burke shut down and could not listen to this girl's story. She says,

> I was horrified by her words. The emotions welling inside of me ran the gamut and I listened until I literally could not take it anymore . . . which turned out to be less than five minutes. Then, right in the middle of her sharing her pain with me, I cut her off and immediately directed her to another female counselor who could help her better.
>
> I will never forget the look on her face. I will never forget the look because I think about her all of the time. The shock of being rejected, the pain of opening a wound only to have it abruptly forced closed again—it was all in her face. I watched her walk away from me as she tried to recapture her secrets and tuck them back into their hiding place. I watched her put her mask back on and go back in the world like she was all alone and I couldn't even bring myself to whisper . . . me too.[9]

Despite turning away from this girl, ultimately, Burke found an opening for connection in the courage these young girls demonstrated when they faced their trauma. Through these experiences, she found herself confronting her own apparently unresolved trauma and realized that healing is a painstakingly slow process that requires the practice of attention. She would later discover that the power of deep listening—being present without judgment or reaction—is critical to healing trauma, one's own and others. Without deep listening, fostering alliances built on trust is virtually impossible. By shifting the dominant cultural views of sexual violence away from stigmatizing girls as victims and, instead, encouraging them to connect with one another, Burke recognized that healing was possible. Healing is possible when the toxic criticism that can trigger shame and self-hatred is eliminated.

Learning from her own experience, Burke saw that emotional patterns interrupt the ability to connect and stay connected with others. Building strong connections with others is the cornerstone to constructing a solid foundation for healing work and reducing the impact of trauma. Myspace, an interactive social media website, became the place where these young girls connected online and shared their stories of sexual violence. Seeing the beauty of black and brown bodies reflected in one another, they experienced a measure of safety and affirmation previously unknown to them. The process of healing began when they claimed their realities and refused to let others shape their identities. They were not victims; they were survivors of sexual violence.

After a Twitter post by actress Alyssa Milano on October 15, 2017, #MeToo went viral. Although Burke had coined the phrase "Me Too" back in 2003, it was Milano's tweet that received global attention and underscored the presence of black women as invisible survivors in all communities.[10] Milano's post encouraged women who had experienced sexual violence to add "#MeToo" to their Twitter status to gauge the prevalence of sexual violence among women. What began as a gesture to raise awareness drew an unprecedented response from women globally. Allegations of sexual abuse in the entertainment industry and the consequences of those allegations soon followed. Like Tarana Burke, Milano attempted to create a platform for women to call attention to sexual violence without making their personal stories public. When the post went viral, Burke was thrust into the spotlight, reminding us that #MeToo had begun in communities of color and for the benefit of underresourced young black girls.

Since the explosion of the #MeToo movement in the news and on social media, Burke has articulated the broader vision of building a coalition of survivors and advocates at the forefront of creating solutions to interrupt the destructive consequences of sexual violence. Among these initiatives, education and advocacy are critical to facilitating healing of survivors and preventing assault.

CONNECTING TO SELF, CONNECTING TO OTHERS

Those of us who struggle with trauma often find it difficult to manage the stress of everyday life. When my mother died, I was inconsolable. Several weeks after the funeral, I was depressed. Friends reached out to comfort me, but it was difficult to accept their care. The rawness of my grief was palpable. One close friend suggested that I attend a retreat at Insight Meditation Society in Barre, Massachusetts. Although I was new to meditation, I was familiar with silent retreats from the days when I was a practicing Catholic. I registered for the next seven-day retreat and put it in my calendar. I had no idea what I was stepping into. As the retreat approached, feelings of sadness gave way to curiosity about what I might learn during a week of intensive meditation. Could meditation bring calmness to the inner chatter that dominated my thoughts? Could sitting quietly help me become aware of the feelings and sensations in my body that often caught me off guard? I was grieving the loss of my mother, and I was terrified that I might become so overwhelmed by depression that I would lose myself.

I settled into the retreat and focused on following the daily structure of sitting and walking meditation. As I sat on the cushion, my thoughts gradually settled. I was wrapped in a warm silence that brought me to tears, releasing a deep well of pain. Throughout the week, I concentrated on my breath and watched my thoughts come and go, feeling brief moments of freedom. Learning *metta*, or lovingkindness practice, helped me to tolerate the noise that filled my head and cope with my own judgments about them. Though I struggled at times, by the end of the retreat,

I was no longer afraid of the passing noise in my head and welcomed the silence as a refuge.

In the weeks after the retreat, I began a daily meditation practice and was determined to find a therapist to help me deal with my grief. Working with a therapist who is trained in trauma work is critical to healing. When I had started a doctoral program in clinical psychology a few years earlier, we were strongly encouraged to find a therapist, but finding a therapist who could understand my experience as a black, queer woman was challenging. Friends and colleagues helped me find people they trusted, and I met each therapist before I committed to therapy with that person. As you can imagine, this process took time but empowered me to find someone who was not just well-trained but who was also human enough to bear witness to the suffering in my black body.

It took me years to recognize that feeling invisible, broken, and unworthy were parts of my experience being repeated from a history of intergenerational trauma. Traumatic memories don't have a beginning, middle, and end. They can be triggered any time, including during meditation. On the one hand, for some people, meditation may not be helpful. According to Dr. Willoughby Britton, a researcher at Brown University, "Meditation can lead people to some dark places, triggering trauma or leaving people feeling disoriented."[11] Britton has studied the adverse effects of meditation on people who have had distressing experiences and found that they can show up even in people who do not experience mental illness. She suggests that people who experience adverse traumatic reactions to meditation focus on mindful actions as an alternative practice.

On the other hand, for many, meditation provides a path to resilience and strengthens body and mind. One meditation practice that I have found helpful is the benefactor practice developed by Dr. John Makransky.[12] Makransky is a Tibetan Buddhist meditation teacher, scholar, and author of *Awakening Through Love: Unveiling Your Deepest Goodness*. His work has focused on adapting traditional Tibetan meditation practices of love and compassion for secular application in social service and interfaith settings. The practice begins by identifying a benefactor, someone in your life who sees your goodness, loves and accepts you unconditionally, and wants the best for you. Benefactors can be teachers, friends, ancestors, mentors, coaches, ministers, or neighbors. Benefactors may be spiritual leaders or public figures, like Martin Luther King Jr., Harriet Tubman, Mahatma Gandhi, Barack Obama, or Audre Lorde, whose presence in the world inspires or motivates you. As you use this practice, more benefactors from your past may come to mind, creating a field of loving support on your behalf. When I offer this practice, I begin by recalling my black, enslaved ancestors as a field of unconditional loving care, resistance, and models of liberation, and I dwell in their presence. You can personalize the practice by, for example, using music, poetry, and journaling along with meditation, creating your own sacred time and space.

INSTRUCTIONS FOR BENEFACTOR PRACTICE

Find a comfortable place on your cushion or chair with your back straight, eyes gazing gently downward.

Begin by taking three slow, deep breaths from your abdomen, pausing slightly between each breath. Allow whatever feelings, thoughts, and sensations arise and notice where they are present in the body. Continue to breathe deeply until the breath settles into a natural rhythm.

Call to mind a benefactor or caring figure who is a source of love and inspiration to you. This person may be in your life, someone who has died, or someone you do not know but who inspires you.

Imagine your benefactor or caring person with you now, not as a memory, but present with you. Standing beside you.

Sense them smiling at you with deep admiration and unconditional love, seeing your goodness beyond any limiting thoughts you may have about who you are.

Stay with this image for a while. Relax in your benefactor's radiant light, allowing this light to soothe any tension you feel in your body or any anxiety or worry.

Rest in the light and let it fully engulf you, receiving this love and communing with your benefactor.

After a few minutes, slowly allow the images of your benefactors to dissolve and fade away.

Continue to sit and let your whole body be infused with their love and compassion for you.

Rest in this moment and after a few minutes, bring the practice to an end.

The benefactor practice weaves together the threads of ancestral myth, memory, and connection with others, all of which may be modes of healing intergenerational trauma that lives in our bodies. Integrating these threads is a lifelong process that can be supported by bringing our benefactors into our meditation practice. We know trauma lives in the body. We carry it every day. Trauma cannot be buried, ignored, pushed aside, or denied. As long as we breathe, trauma reminds us it is with us and rises to the surface. Transforming trauma means being willing to address it in our lives. Developing a daily practice helps us to be with whatever comes up and not shut down.

Several years ago, I was on a weekend retreat in New Hampshire during the summer and met Lama Rod Owens for the first time. He had just completed a three-year silent retreat at Kagyu Thubten Chöling Monastery outside of New York City and received authorization to teach from his root teacher, Venerable Lama Norlha Rinpoche. With this authorization, he became a *lama*, or teacher, in the Kagyu school of Tibetan Buddhism. I remember nervously leaving him a note to ask if we could meet after the retreat. When the retreat ended, we took a walk along an old, winding road near the retreat center. It was hot and I was sweating profusely, and I was anxious about making myself vulnerable to someone I hardly knew. Breathlessly, I blurted out that I struggled with depression my entire life and asked him if he believed meditation could make a difference.

Without hesitation, he spoke in a soft voice about the impact of intergenerational trauma on black and brown bodies, and encouraged me to sit every day, even when I was feeling depressed.

He listened to me; I knew he was familiar with my struggle. But through regular spiritual practice, he had found freedom from the darkness that had haunted him and was haunting me at the time. Through meditation, he said, eventually feelings of depression would find open space and develop into equanimity, or mental calmness. By learning to sit with discomfort, you develop an ability to be with whatever feelings, sensations, and thoughts arise within the body with presence and the courage to be with yourself just as you are in each moment.

Whenever I feel stuck, I return to these words of wisdom from Lama Rod that connect me to a powerful lineage of ancestors. From the myths of enslaved ancestors to finding connection with others who share similar trauma, there are many tools of healing available to us. Our healing, regardless of how we choose to heal, begins when we have the courage to lead with love and honor those connections as we seek collective liberation.

· 2 ·

THE DHARMA OF TRAUMA

Blackness, Buddhism, and Transhistorical Trauma Narrated through Three Ayahuasca Ceremonies

LAMA ROD OWENS

How I got over
How did I make it over?
You know my soul look back and wonder
How did I make it over?
—"Clara Ward," as sung by ARETHA FRANKLIN

Healing begins where the wound was made.[1]
—ALICE WALKER, *The Way Forward Is with a Broken Heart*

People are trapped in history and history is trapped in them.[2]
—JAMES A. BALDWIN, "Stranger in the Village"

TO BEGIN WITH, the plant medicine, ayahuasca, had been calling me for about two years. I knew nothing about it outside of the criticism people around me had about the medicine being more a psychedelic, perhaps the lazy person's spiritual practice. Maybe this was my opinion as well.

I had been hearing of ayahuasca groups happening all over

(particularly in Brooklyn with "urban shamans") for years but it was something that just didn't appeal to me. Though I knew little about it at that time, I knew drinking it in the wild energetic vibrations of New York City didn't feel safe for me.

I ended up attending the 2018 Buddhist Teachers of African Descent gathering at Union Theological Seminary with my home-girl and fellow dharma teacher, Spring Washam. I knew Spring was leading ayahuasca retreats in Peru. Matter of fact, it was the hush-hush gossip among dharma teachers. Her work seemed subversive and controversial—two words I find evocative and full of creativity. At the gathering, she told me about her extensive experience with ayahuasca, including retreats she ran down in Peru, guiding groups through ceremonies.[3] I was intrigued and knew that I wanted to join her September 2019 retreat, which, auspiciously, would begin on my fortieth birthday. I knew I was being summoned to be in relationship with it.

It is said that one should not approach ayahuasca with an agenda or goals, but with pure, positive intention. My intention was to go down to the Peruvian Amazon to mourn the first forty years of my life. I wanted to let go of what I didn't need any longer and step into this new phase of my life. I wasn't sure how that was going to happen, but I decided to enter into the process with an open heart and mind.

WHAT IS AYAHUASCA?

Ayahuasca is often thought of as a psychedelic drug. However, my experience of the ayahuasca was that it is a *medicine*, and among the communities who have been working with ayahuasca seriously—including native, indigenous cultures in the Amazon basin whose healing culture is based on the plant—it is referred to as a medicine. From this point on, I also refer to it as a medicine.

Ayahuasca is considered a medicine because of how it purges both the body and the mind. Anyone with experience with the medicine knows there is quite a bit of purging in the form of vomiting and diarrhea. Before and after a ceremony, you are expected to observe a strict, cleansing diet, which further detoxes the body.

Ayahuasca as a medicine is actually a combination of two plants: the ayahuasca vine and one of several other plants with which it is traditionally brewed. The medicine used in my ceremonies was a combination of ayahuasca and the *chacruna* shrub. The contents of the ayahuasca vine are scraped out and placed in a pot with the chacruna leaves and boiled down to a thick tea.

THE CEREMONIES

When you sit and drink the medicine, that is called a ceremony. When the medicine begins to take effect, that is called a journey. My cohort's ceremonies were guided by a local shaman named Maestro Adriano of the Shipibo people, along with Spring, our maestra. We held our ceremonies in a group in the ceremonial space called the *moloka*. Ceremonies began around 8 p.m. most nights and ended around 1:30 a.m.

What made the ceremonies particularly powerful was the use of the *ikaro*. The ikaro is a song derived from the consciousness of plants. An ikaro can be specific for the person whom it is being sung to. Maestro Adriano would sing ikaro for each of us individually with the assistance of Spring. The ikaro isn't just a song but a way in which the maestro sings to the medicine inside of you. My experience of this felt like the ikaro was activating the medicine I had drunk in a way that helped the medicine to focus and become more potent. I often had very strong reactions to the ikaro being sung to me.

In ceremonies, the medicine expresses itself as a voice of wisdom and support; this voice is different for different people. For me, the medicine expressed itself as the Mother, experienced as a deep consciousness of nurturing, care, and stability. The Mother is also the expression of Shakti, the feminine energy of the universe experienced as love. The Mother would take on different masks: sometimes as my teachers, sometimes as people who loved me, and then other times as a direct voice manifesting in my consciousness. The Mother was always present with me as a guide.

I have decided to share my experience of three of the seven ceremonies from the retreat because these ceremonies speak directly to what I originally wanted to explore in this writing—trauma. Sharing my experiences of working with the trauma in these ceremonies is important because they helped me to do something that no practice in Buddhism had helped me to do prior. It is important for me to say that Buddhism doesn't hold all the paths and keys for me; there are so many other paths, wisdoms, and modalities that are important for us to explore.

As a Black, queer dharma teacher, I am beginning to value the indigenous wisdom of my African and slave ancestors, who are strong with me. When we begin to value and celebrate our ancestors, we naturally begin to incorporate their way of being into our lives. We also are reintroduced to their spirituality and their deities, which has been a very welcomed surprise for me. I want my Blackness to be supported by my dharma practice, not erased by it. I think that this was one of the teachings I was supposed to understand from the ceremonies.

This retreat, especially these three ceremonies, were some of the hardest experiences I have ever had. Even as I write this, I am still deep in recovery and integration. I am hovering between seeing the benefits and regretting the whole thing. I feel that this is all natural to the process of deep, transformative work.

THE DEMONS OF BLACK FOLKS

I often interpret trauma as a demon, and I understand transhistorical racial trauma as a demon that has possessed the bodies, minds, and spirits of slave-descended folks for hundreds of years.

When I am speaking of trauma, I am often speaking of the disembodiment that happens because of a violent or harsh experience. This disrupts how we relate to ourselves and thus establish a pattern of modified behaviors when encountering the experience that triggered the original disruption. Trauma can be either physical or emotional. We misuse the term "trauma" in vague attempts to describe some form of suffering. Trauma is not just getting our feelings hurt or having a tough experience. A traumatic experience is an experience that knocks you out of your body and makes it difficult for you to return back to the body. And because of this disruption, our physical and emotional sensations frequently do not line up with what's happening around us.

Trauma impacts all expressions of our body, which results in a disruption in our feeling that the world and our experiences are safe for us. We are altered in ways we do not recognize. Trauma is like riding on a train heading to a destination on a route you are familiar with. Then something happens and the train changes tracks at an intersection, now heading somewhere different. Trauma is very much this changing of the tracks. You've gotten on a different path without realizing it, something happens, then you notice that the route you are on has become unfamiliar—but you don't know why or how to get back on the right track.

The train analogy makes it easier to picture an individual's experience with trauma, but how do we approach understanding the trauma that transcends an individual's experience or even the traumatic experiences of a single generation? Transhistorical trauma is trauma that moves from generation to generation—until it is disrupted and released from the ancestral or collective line.

For most Black Americans, the root of transhistorical intergenerational trauma is the grueling and brutal transatlantic slave journey called the Middle Passage. The Middle Passage has been widely taught and studied as a historical artifact, safely tucked away in the past. However, as I stepped out of my first forty years of life, I would be called to confront the wounds of the Middle Passage in an intimate way.

IN COMES THE SPIDER

On the first night of ceremony, my journey takes me where I know I need to go—into a part of my consciousness that seems to be possessed.

Maestro's ikaro *triggers a deep and heavy purging. I vomit up a bitter fluid from my stomach into the small buckets we keep beside our mats in the* moloka. *I have the strange feeling that part of my consciousness has split and found its way to hell and that what I am vomiting is more than my own physical purging.*

After my purging with the maestro, I am helped outside to get some fresh air and feel the earth under me. Lying outside in the Amazon jungle, under a moon that seems ancient, surrounded by swaying trees and plants that are no doubt trying to communicate with me, I drift in and out of consciousness. I find myself waking with the sensation of what feels like an insect crawling on my arm. I habitually flick it off, and immediately after I do, I hear something in my ear begin to chuckle. This catches my attention.

"What are you?" I ask into the night air. The response is not so direct. Initially, there is no voice speaking to me but just impressions running through my mind. These impressions slowly begin to form a word, sound by sound. The first sound that becomes clear is an "An" followed by a "Ni" and finally "Say." I speak the name aloud: "Anisée." I know whom I have made contact with: it is the African spider god, Anansi. It feels strange to me to be so clearly discerning Anisée. Am I mistaken? No—the deity makes himself clearer to me and lets me call him Anisée.

After this introduction, Anisée becomes more and more direct, to the point where we are communicating directly with each other. I speak verbally or mentally with him, and he responds through impressions embedded right in my stream of consciousness. Anisée would become a guide for me in the second ceremony and be supportive through the remaining ceremonies.

"KEEP YOUR JOY"

My second ceremony begins with my slave ancestors gathering around me. As they sit staring at me, they reflect a hardness that feels rigid and cold. I know they are angry. I know that they are enraged. I wonder what they want from me. Being a well-trained Buddhist, I decide that I will offer them lovingkindness in the form of sharing joy with them. As I am attempting to wish for their happiness and freedom from suffering, they interrupt me, speaking in one voice: "Keep your joy. We don't need your joy. We need you to witness."

As is true for many Black folks, my experience of "rage" goes beyond the normal sense of that word (a kind of uncontrolled anger) into the territory of transhistorical rage—the shadow of intergenerational trauma. Black rage rides the breath of transhistorical trauma. Both ride together as a highly functional and detrimental pair. Both trauma and rage have been a part of how I have come to relate to Blackness. While I do believe that Blackness is full of great joy, I also admit that it is full of a potent sorrow. Trauma and rage live in the heart of this potent sorrow.

I define Black rage as a disembodied expression of deep disappointment that longs to be cared for. This deep disappointment is not just my suffering in this life but also the suffering of all my ancestors. The path of healing is practicing embodiment—to return home to all my bodies—and do the very hard work of loving the trauma. And by loving it, we begin to set it free from our bodies. The rage is anger that has compounded through generation after generation of struggling to be well in racism, patriarchy, and capitalism—systems that rob not just Black folks but all people of vitality, vision, breath, and space. The rage is also the frustration of never feeling as if there is enough when there are others who have much more than they could possibly ever need.

When we experience rage, we understand that we are experiencing the rage of all our ancestors. When we experience love, we are also experiencing the love of all our ancestors. Transhistorical love—often felt as resilience—is what keeps me and many of us alive. When we fall deeply into the love that we are being gifted, then we begin to thrive, and thriving disrupts the systems of violence that were only created to annihilate us. We disrupt these systems because we survive them—a system of violence that does not kill us has failed. We summon our joy and dance into our thriving. We are our ancestors' wildest dreams because we thrive.

THAT DARK SICK PLACE

After my ancestors leave me, I sit cross-legged, peering down into my puke bucket, into a portal that leads into the guts of what I have understood my whole life to be: hell. I know I have to journey to the bottom of this ship. There are sounds of moaning and puking on top of the creaking of a ship hurtling itself across an ocean. I feel the color crimson as both heat and an experience of something evil. I feel sharp anxiety arise, and I begin to resist. "No, no, no," I think to myself. "Not tonight." By then the maestro is sitting in front of me to sing his ikoros *to me. I lose my agency. Even though I feel myself resisting, I am already there.*

In the ship, I am an adolescent girl, lying on a platform next to other bodies. The heat of the space is saturated with the bitter tanginess of vomit and the earthy, nauseating stench of shit and piss. There is a subtle hint of a metallic blood. People are dead and dying. I think I am lying next to someone who has died. Around me, I hear the moaning, sometimes a scream. Anisée is somewhere in the shadows. Somehow, the medicine is keeping me from fully falling into the brutality of this experience. What I am experiencing is enough, and at the same time, it is too much.

I do not know what to do. Somehow, I am holding all the people— my ancestors—in my mind, and I confess to them that I have no idea what to do. Yet, I do the only thing I know how to do: take on all the suffering in that dark sick place. I tell my ancestors to give their pain to me. Slowly, I begin to feel the energy of intense suffering and pain collect in my stomach, filling it up as if I am pregnant. I imagine myself sitting up in a pool of blood, piss, shit, and sweat, grasping my big, swollen stomach, taking in more and more of this suffering. In the moment, I keep thinking that this isn't enough, but it is all I know how to do.

ON BLACKNESS AND ANGER

Although Black anger is part of the Black experience, Blackness and anger are not the same thing. This has taken me years to understand. Blackness, for me, is an identity location that articulates my race and my ancestral roots in Africa. It is also a political identity that speaks of how those like me have survived systematic violence, marginalization, and cultural erasure in a social context that was created to use my body for production and now sees my body as expendable. I believe the Movement for Black Lives emerged to highlight this violence while at the same time seeking to restore value and care to the lives of Black folks. Yet, this political Blackness also embraces the lives of all people who survive systems of racial violence. My identity as being Black means I am always on the side of those of us who are targeted by systematic violence including racism, queerphobia, transphobia, misogyny, ableism, and ageism. A personal slogan of mine is that if you are marginalized, you are Black.

Although Blackness and anger are not the same thing, my experience as a Black person has been riddled with racial trauma, and trauma and anger ride together often. The anger is a reaction to the suffering I experience being Black and targeted, with very little relief. Not only am I struggling with my own trauma in this life, I am also shouldering the burden of the trauma that has been passed to me from my ancestors. Each generation has had to hold the pain of the previous generation; in holding it, the pain becomes ours even though we have no idea where it comes from. It is passed down because those before us have not had the capacity to heal or understand their trauma, which sets the conditions for it to be transmitted to the next generation. It is as simple as a parent passing it to a child. I believe that any racialized person is a traumatized person, as racialization is a socially imposed experience with socially constructed meanings that disrupt our ability to receive the resources we need to be emotionally healthy. But not all experiences of racialization are equivalent. My experience growing up racialized as Black has meant dealing with the suffering of racism.

When I first starting practicing meditation, I had to confront anger. Even early on in my practice, I knew that my anger was important, that it was connected to the pain I was experiencing having been raised Black in this country. Yet when I started getting space around my anger, I found myself experiencing a productive struggle in my relationship to Blackness. As I started doing the practices and experiencing so much spaciousness in my mind around the anger, I felt concerned by the possibility that I was becoming less Black! This spaciousness resulted in feeling settled, which began to directly disrupt my perception of how I am Black—and many other things. In other words, I discovered that being Black-identified does not mean that I am also anger-identified. To be Black has come with significant woundedness and trauma from having to survive a white supremacist culture as well as having to hold the transhistorical trauma of my ancestors who also survived the same trauma and passed it on unknowingly to me. Yet because of my meditation practice, I have an experience of Blackness that is based upon resiliency, community, deep joy in the face of violence, and a profound gratitude for my culture, which continues to transform marginalization into celebration. My trauma and anger are still parts of this celebration, but they are not what Blackness means. They are only some of the consequences of being in this system.

"WHAT ABOUT THE CHILDREN?"

I am in the guts of that sick place, barely surviving, barely remembering my name, exhausted, enraged, done with the world and its evil and its sick, cold white men. Somewhere above, I am nuzzled in the arms of Spring, who is gently asking me to remember my breath and return to my body. I need to return to my body. I need to get the fuck out of here. I am convinced that my work is done for the night.

"No." Anisée, in his spider form, exclaims as he spins around on a thin string to face me.

"No?" I respond, wanting to tell him to go fuck off.

"No. What about the children?"

"What children?"

"The innocent little ones who do not deserve to be here. The little ones who were stolen from their lives to lie rotting in this filth."

Suddenly, children start emerging from the darkness of the bowels of the ship. I find myself collapsing to the floor in the darkness as the children curl up around me. I stretch out my hands to cover them.

"You are the Father," I hear whispered from somewhere behind me. The rage and grief come upon me with such violence that I go numb. In that numbness, a new vision opens up. Looking around me at the children, I begin to see that their playful, sweet innocence starts to fade, slowly being replaced by a dry grayness that renders them like zombies. In that moment, I know that I have seen the genesis of transhistorical trauma.

Knowing that I have seen this, they look up at me and speak in a collective voice:

"This is what we have given to you. You are just like us. You are us. But there is a difference with you. You have learned how to fight the darkness."

It seems to take lifetimes to understand that revelation. These sweet, innocent babies. My babies.

Again, somewhere in the background: "You are the Father."

"What about the other children?" Anisée whispers.

"What other children?"

"The children from other races and civilizations whose innocence was taken away by the cruelty of adults."

And slowly, as if the sun were rising, the bottom of that sick place fills with light and I begin to see groups of young people walking toward me. I have the impression that there are young people from times and places outside of any history that has ever been recorded. However, the children coming closest to me are from this time and place, children who I know and can name and cry for.

First come the children of the Holocaust, who appear as thin, skeleton-like beings with sunken, light-gray eyes and ashy-white skin. Most are Jewish but not all of them. They wear what look like white pajamas with vertical stripes of gray and black. Behind them are American Indian children covered in blood. Their bodies are riddled with scars and bruises. I can't really see their faces. Yet with a few I can see at least one eye exposed, and those eyes seem to protrude through streams of blood, bulging with the energy of horror. Next come the Japanese and Chinese children of American work camps, internment camps, and indentured servitude. They come almost as gray and silent shadows who seem to just stare through me. More children come, and as they come and sit with my ancestors, I understand that these visions of them are the expressions of trauma that they, too, passed on to their progeny in the same way my ancestors explained.

THE WILDFIRE OF INTERGENERATIONAL TRAUMA

Our trauma and its rage began with the forced capture, bondage, and transportation of between ten and fifteen million Africans, with about two million dying during some part of this experience.[4] Our ancestors were chained and packed in the bowels of cargo ships, where they experienced an overwhelming variety of physical and mental ailments. Those who survived the trauma of the passage were introduced into what was to be centuries of forced enslavement, resulting in a deep and brutal impact on the Black body and mind.

Yet, the Middle Passage represents much more than the transport of Black bodies across an ocean; it was and still is the trauma of decisions made without consent. It is the creation of a context that does not privilege one's deepest desire to return home and inhabit one's own agency and body. It is the perpetuation of a context that triggers disembodiment, making out of Black bodies, minds, and spirits the meanings that fulfill the intentions of a racist and capitalist imagination. Thus, trauma in this context becomes a cyclical experience of continuous unfolding, of continuous forced movement without consent. It perpetuates terror, despair, hopelessness, and disconnection. It is a voyage that never docks at any port but remains suspended, unexamined.

The trauma that Africans experienced was transmitted to their children and onward through successive generations through the practice of storytelling, through belief and value transfers, and through behavior, which affected how each generation of African Americans related to their own bodies, minds, and to other groups.[5] And the trauma was not just passed down but also renewed and perpetuated with the oppression of systematic racism. Thus, transhistorical intergenerational trauma can be likened to a wildfire spreading through a forest. Though the fire no longer exists at its point of origin, it still continues to spread and is aided by the conditions of dry, burning material and wind. The Middle Passage is the spark, the original trauma, that is now lost in the past. Black Americans are the forest and our trauma symptoms, the fire. The dry materials are retraumatizing factors—periods like Jim Crow, lynch culture, and instances like police brutality and microaggressions. And systemized oppression and racism is the wind keeping the fire spreading.

The Middle Passage is a symbol of the precise point of trauma that has influenced the psychic development of slaves and their descendants. It is the impact of terror, paranoia, stress, despair, and deeply compromised self-esteem that is perpetuated by systematic racism and oppression.

THE WOMEN GATHER CRYING

This is what my dharma is tonight: As I sit on the side of my bed, and without consent, my heart breaks. It shatters. In the shattering, the big, warm watermelon tears fall. I try to collect them in my hands. They are too much for me to hold. This is when the women gather around. They are my mothers, grandmothers, lovers, sister kinfolks, and girl cousins. They come and hold me, and in the holding, they tell me stories of how they have been mourning since before the trauma, since before they came and took our little ones and fed them into the guts of the floating demons. They have been crying the most desperate tears, laced with the most profound love.

"But has this love saved our people?" I ask in between sobs.

"No, our tears have saved no one, not even the little ones. We do not cry to save anyone. We cry on behalf of our family, especially the ones who have forgotten how to cry. We mourn the mourning that is lost to them. You are one of us. We are the crying Mothers. You now become the crying Father."

With that acknowledgment, I surrender and roll over in tears and grief into the laps of the Mothers. Together, we mourn our children.

MOURNING THE BROKEN HEART

Mourning has become an important practice for me. I am learning to intentionally mourn. This may sound strange. However, I am noticing that so much of my freedom and joy is bound up in my capacity to mourn things. Mourning is my attempt to acknowledge brokenheartedness, accept it, and offer it space to be in my experience so it may do its work of teaching me and passing through. I am learning how to let myself be with my hurt whenever it comes up, even if it means I have to stop everything that I am doing and support this experience through meditation, breath work, movement, or even tears. Whenever I feel this energy, I allow it, and it is something I am encouraging others to do as well. When we are sitting with someone, it is an expression of compassion to offer them the space to move through their brokenheartedness.

Our woundedness, as it manifests as brokenheartedness, becomes something that we begin to habitually avoid out of our fear that it has power over us. In my practice, I'm trying to be in power *with* my brokenheartedness. I don't want to have power over it. I don't have to have power under it. I want to be in power *with*. And what does that mean to be in power with? It means I meet my woundedness, my discomfort, with a kind of friendliness. This friendliness is a warmth and openness that allows the discomfort to be there. This friendliness is an expression of love, and that love is the energy that opens up the space around the discomfort. When I can notice the space, I can have the room to be in power with my brokenheartedness. In this sense, my discomfort becomes something I can be collaborative with, not overwhelmed by.

If I can meet my brokenheartedness head-on in this collaboration, then the chance I will learn something from my woundedness increases. If I try to control the brokenheartedness, I find myself pushing it away, saying, "I don't want to deal with this." If I find myself being in power under the discomfort, then it becomes overwhelming for me to deal with, and there is no learning.

When I'm in power with, on the same level, I meet it head-on and I'm able to stay aware and attentive to all the aspects of the discomfort as it's happening. Then I am in a better position to learn from and experience the wisdom of my discomfort. The wisdom comes from my ability to experience the discomfort or brokenheartedness. The heart of contemplative practices is about experiencing what's happening and understanding that we can survive the experience if we can connect to the spaciousness that is both in and around our experiences.

If we shut down and get really tight around an experience, we will lose ourselves in the experience, and it will be overwhelming. When we instead get loose and wide around the experience, then the space around the experience has a lot of potential for other things to happen. There's the potentiality for happiness to arise, for contentment to arise. There's the potentiality for other choices to be made in how we relate to discomfort. When there is space around the difficulty, we have agency.

There is a Black mourning that I experience. It is touching into the brutality of what it has meant to occupy a Black body in this life and allowing myself to feel into that discomfort and release it. What holds me in this process is the presence of a deep, vibrant joy that Black folks during our time in captivity on this foreign land have given rise to.

"CHAINS AND SHACKLES"

Between sessions, I found it difficult to walk. My narrative was that the medicine was taking my mobility away. I knew that there was another, more precise explanation. When I was speaking to Spring after the second ceremony, she mentioned seeing energetic chains around my neck as well as my legs. It made sense and felt familiar, like something that I had contemplated before. These chains represented my and other slave-descended folks' bondage in transhistorical trauma. I wondered what I could do to break these chains.

LET MY PEOPLE GO

In the third ceremony, the medicine tells me that this part of my work with the Middle Passage is over. I have done what I have needed to do. Yet, these chains still bother me. I will the medicine to reveal these energetic chains and shackles. They appear as glowing, energetic things that shift between translucent gold and green. I wonder how to break them. The medicine tells me to gather my strength and break them.

So, I begin to gather my strength and embrace an intense sense of authority. I feel like I am becoming some kind of powerful wizard calling into me the energy of my ancestors, family, as well as the purity of my aspirations to be an agent of liberation. I look down at the chains and shackles around my ankles, and say: "On behalf of my ancestors, I break these chains, releasing all of us forever from the demon of this trauma!" Slowly they begin to resolve, and from that moment on I do not have any trouble walking in between ceremonies.

CLOSING SERMON: BREAKING MORE CHAINS AND DISRUPTING A CULTURE OF TRAUMA

Lately, I have been reflecting on how trauma creates culture.

I will start by admitting that the only thing I have ever wanted is to be free. I grew up in the Black church where we were very interested in freedom. One of the stories that we all knew by heart was the Exodus. There are several spirituals in our tradition about the Exodus. Many of our slave ancestors, when they heard that story for the first time, believed that it was about them, about us. We were the children held captive in a strange land. God wanted to deliver us from our captivity. They knew God would send a Moses, and he did—several times over. Sometimes we called her Harriet. Once, even Nat Turner. He was called Lincoln eventually as well.

God sent Moses to deliver the children of Israel out of Egypt. He parted the sea and marched his people into freedom, which was an exile of wandering until they were prepared to enter the promised land. It seems like Black folks experienced the same. Once our people were freed, we entered the long, violent exile of Jim Crow, segregation, and lynching, which continued to perpetuate our trauma and devalue our lives. God has sent many Moseses, and maybe what we called Moses is now Black Lives Matter. As a former Christian turned Buddhist, this is my understanding of liberation theology. I understand this theology to mean that God is on the side of the oppressed and He makes a promise to free all those who remain faithful to Him.[6] Those who practice goodness are always walking in the light, no matter how dark it is.

I think so much of our liberation begins with listening to how we are being told to be free. When my mother began listening, she started saying, "Show me what to do. Show me how to serve, how to follow You." As a preteen, looking at that, I saw something that was, can I say, revolutionary. As she stepped into the ministry in the United Methodist Church, she showed me how to show up as a person of faith, regardless of everyone telling you not to do what you need to do.

Though I am a Black *lama* (Tibetan Buddhist teacher), in my heart is the Black church. The Black church has represented for me the strategy to disrupt the workings of oppression, white supremacy, and all the various nuanced and subtle ways in which this country, individuals, communities, systems, and institutions have contrived to exterminate Black-bodied people, in the same way they have tried to exterminate our indigenous people of this country. However, we have survived by using our faith, songs, magic, and most importantly, our love and joy. This lies at the heart of resiliency.

When I remember this resiliency, I am remembering my grandfather, who was also a minister. His legal name was actually Moses. Remembering him, I remember myself. So much of the work is about remembering who and what I am with the help of my ancestors. Remembering that I am not what people tell me that I am, and remembering that I am not what I see on TV about who I am. First and foremost, I remember myself as a person who is the essence of love, who is the essence of God, and who is the essence of the Mother. However we conceive of God and divinity, we are that. We are not our mistakes, we are not the violence that we manifest, and we are not our despair. We are not our sadness. We are joy. When we take part in that remembering and that stepping into that joy, what we're actually doing is practicing liberation. We're practicing a revolution. How can we remember that?

We're connected to a lineage of ancestry. For Black folks, one of the things that keeps us oppressed and marginalized is the belief that we don't belong anywhere or to anything. There has never really been a place for us in this country and nor have we ever been told we have a right to agency over our bodies. We start believing these things, and we start teaching our children, and before long, we are collectively passing it on to the next generation of young people. That's one of the reasons I started working with youth; I felt like they were being told to forget who they were and where they came from. To remember the ancestors, to remember their history, is a deeply basic way that we begin to interrogate oppression. All the elders, the prophets—especially our contemporary prophets and elders—keep telling us the same thing over and over again: "Remember. Remember who you are." What does that mean for you? What does it mean when I say, "Who are you?" What are you and what do you stand for?

We're afraid to remember who we are because we've been told it's not our right to do. There's another part of that too. Not only are we being told to forget but we're also being told that we don't have a right to be in our bodies, to own our bodies, have agency over our bodies. You see that over and over again. Once we begin to remember our history in this social context of this country, we see that our lack of agency, our lack of being at home in our bodies, has produced so much violence and despair. When our ancestors were abducted and brought to this land, what was happening in that transatlantic slave trade was not just a transportation but also a breaking of the relationship to our own bodies. It was a violent enactment of the message that we were no longer ourselves. That's what they told us, and then we believed it.

The Dharma of Gospel or the Truth about the Good News

I remember the sorrow songs. "Sorrow song"—when I first heard this phrase, a sadness came over me, and I began to shiver. It was something I couldn't articulate. On occasion, the slave ship's crew would bring groups of the captured Africans above deck to wash them. They were chained together in small groups. These small groups were often from the same village, so they shared the same language and could communicate with each other, and sometimes they would decide to jump overboard into the ocean. The song was one of mourning, the sorrow song. I think about that often. I think about what I would do if I were faced with being enslaved for the rest of my life. How would I choose to be free? There's no judgment there; it's not a moral issue. There is just a simple question: what can I allow myself to endure before I choose freedom, whatever freedom is?

So much of what I understand to be liberatory is really about remembering my body and remembering that my body is the result of many people, decisions, and acts that have come before me. My body is not only the result of love and celebration, but also despair. How do we connect to that as people? Not just brown people, but white people, Asian people, whomever? How can we connect to our histories, our lineages, and not connect necessarily to the violence or the despair but to that liberatory joy within the body? To do that means we have to negotiate the compounded and collective trauma in our own bodies—and that's the work. That's the work when we leave home, and we come back, and we see our home is all messed up. We come back home into our bodies, we begin to do the work, and that's really where I come from.

I believe *dharma* is very similar to the word *gospel* that we use in biblical studies. *Gospel* means the good news and *dharma* means teachings of the Buddha, the law, or any law teaching the truth. I understand dharma also to be gospel—the good news, the good news of being freed, of being liberated. Turning that attention back into ourselves, into our own minds, into our own despair, and liberating ourselves from the chains of despair.

INSTRUCTIONS FOR BENEFACTOR PRACTICE

I want to invite you into a short practice with me. Draw your attention into your body. Where is your attention being drawn to in the body? Just look. As you're looking, and if you are able to, take one hand and place it just on the chest, on your heart center, around the heart. Just notice the hand on your chest. I want you to feel what it's like to touch your own body.

Feel each finger on your chest, that individual feeling, sensation, and pressure of each finger against the chest. Feel the palm of the hand. This is your body. It's not my body, it's not the police's body, it's not the government's body. It's your body. As you connect to the sense of your body, look at some of the more uncomfortable things that come up for you. Look at some of the discomforts, some of the unpleasant emotions, feelings, sensations that come up. You're not doing anything about it, but just looking. You're acknowledging. So much of our liberation is really about accepting. You can't liberate yourself from something you can't accept.

As you're connecting to your body, I want you to ask yourself a question: What do I need right now? As you ask this question, see what comes up. I'll challenge you as you ask this question not to actually answer it—at least not with your mind. Allow your body, your spirit, to answer the question. Allow the spirit to arise. Allow the body to answer and notice.

Just let your spirit, let your body answer that. Just be with whatever comes. Try not to sit there and think, "Oh, this is what I need." As you are listening for what's coming, what's being offered to you, imagine and maybe visualize in front of you, in any way that you choose, a being, a spirit, or God. Anything, any being that is a source of compassion and love for you. Be it your understanding of God, be it your understanding of Christ, or the Buddha, or an ancestor, or someone you've loved very much—a mother, a father, a sister or brother, any deity. Any being or divine presence that is nothing but love and compassion for you. Imagine, somehow, that you are in the presence of this being. I want you to feel that. I want you to lean into this energy of love from what we are calling, now, the benefactor, your benefactor.

Can you feel that? Can you sense it? What is it like for you to be loved? What is it like for you to be seen? As you lean into this love from the benefactor, imagine that you're asking your benefactor right now to offer to you, to give to you, what you most need right now. Simply allow that benefactor to offer what you need at this very moment, in whatever form that takes. Not thinking about it, not conceptualizing, but allowing the benefactor to offer you what you need.

Now, let go of holding the presence of the benefactor with you, allowing the benefactor to dissolve into, perhaps, white light, and allowing that light to be absorbed through your hands, right into your own heart. The benefactor will continue to offer you what you need. As you continue to receive what you need, I invite you to offer a prayer right now, praying that all people right now, all beings in the world—all animals, all humans, all spirits, all divine creatures— somehow receive what they most need right now. If you're interested in being a saint or bodhisattva, make an extra prayer, and pray that you become what those around you need when they need it.

Amen.

DEDICATION

I dedicate this chapter to my ancestors. I also remember Anansi, known to me as Anisée, who sang to the children and loved them in the darkness. May we all be free.

· 3 ·

TURNING TOWARD MYSELF

SEBENE SELASSIE

Autobiography is a wound where the blood of history does not dry.[1]
— GAYATRI CHAKRAVORTY SPIVAK, "Acting Bits/Identity Talk"

…the function, the very serious function of racism is
distraction. It keeps you from doing your work. It keeps you
explaining, over and over again, your reason for being.
—TONI MORRISON

The Path will go on
rising and falling
like a song—
and in the end
you will find yourself
as one lost at sea
finds herself
finally washed ashore.
—*THE FIRST FREE WOMEN*, translated by Matty Weingast

BLACK AND BUDDHIST are two designations not without complication for me. Though the former is denominated and the latter adopted, both are fiction. Each is a concept used to describe lives, cultures, and realities much too complex for a single word. Yet, for many years I considered myself equally not Black enough and not Buddhist enough. Rather than abandon Blackness and Buddhism because they are social constructs, I choose to live them: explore them, practice them, dispute them, and, ultimately, love them. My relationships with Blackness and Buddhism have been complex, even fraught, but often profound. Buddhism allows me to see the ever-changing being I am. Blackness assures me that there is a glorious ancestry within me. They both espouse joy and freedom. Blackness and Buddhism teach me to love my multiplicities, to love myself.

I did not grow up particularly religious. That is, my family did not attend church regularly. We went maybe only a dozen times throughout my entire childhood, including weddings and funerals. My circle of friends in high school didn't come from religious families either. They usually attended special services (Christmas or bar mitzvahs), if at all. From toddlerhood through early adulthood, I was surrounded by white, middle-class, mostly secular, dominant culture—until I chose to turn toward other things: art, feminism, queerness, postmodernism, postcolonialism and, also, Blackness and Buddhism, which together taught me finally to turn toward myself. I found that I (and each of us) contain much more than this world had me imagine. As Walt Whitman said, "I contain multitudes." And it's in embracing those multitudes that my liberation lies.

I don't remember when I first encountered the idea of being "not Black enough." Probably around the same time I heard the word *Oreo* used as an insult toward Black kids who were perceived as "acting white" and therefore were only Black on the outside. Let me be clear, I did not receive that insult (at least not to my face). Not because I wasn't an Oreo. Most of my American references and connections—music, pop culture, style—were white. By food-as-racial-metaphor standards, I probably *was* an Oreo. But mainly I was an immigrant. Until adulthood, I never spent much time with non-Ethiopian Black people. We had emigrated from Addis Ababa to Washington, DC, in 1974 when I was three. With the exception of our home and our circle of Ethiopian family and friends (and the occasional Eritreans), I spent the majority of my young life surrounded by white people. Yes, in *that* Washington, DC. Upper Northwest DC in the mid-seventies was not Chocolate City on the other side of Rock Creek Park (more and more, no part of DC is). White people made up the majority of Lafayette Elementary School and its surrounding suburban-like streets. Almost all my high school friends were white. Actually, most of my friends from preschool through college were white. It was a reverse-Oreo reality—my Blackness was engulfed by white stuff.

But I didn't think *I'm not Black enough* until my late teens. During my first month at McGill University in Montreal, I attended the Black Students Network orientation for first-year students; I longed to connect to the part of myself that often remained unnamed among my white friends. I entered the room how my introverted self enters all new spaces, curious and shy. I remember feeling particularly anxious and entirely out of place, so it speaks to the depth of my longing that I braved the meeting. The older Black students all knew each other, but even some of the incoming freshman had previous connections. This was a room full of the Canadian version of Black Ivy Leaguers. Instead of pastel Ralph Lauren Polo shirts, they had richly colored *Roots* sweaters.

I, on the other hand, wore my dad's old gray wool overcoat, my absolute coolest vintage item. Compared to the other students, I felt ragged. The meeting had an agenda item identifying local salons, which threw me off. I had never been to a Black hair salon in my life. I was the only woman with long, messy, natural hair (this was 1988, before the natural hair re-revolution of Afro Punk and curly hair products at chain drugstores). My mother had always discouraged me from straightening my hair and cut it herself, which is why I always had weird hair. And that was maybe the least weird thing about me. I was a Black teen who wore secondhand clothing, read palms, quoted Monty Python sketches, and listened to Ska music. Up to this point in my life, I'd always managed to find other weirdos (usually white). This room full of bright, fashionable, Canadian Black people did not seem to be my people. Rather than simply acknowledge my difference, what I believed was *I am not Black enough.*

Enough is the qualifier. I'd never longed to be white and was often reminded I could not be. A week earlier, I had been walking down the street in this unfamiliar city and was called a nigger. That wasn't the first time I'd had that word screamed at me by white people; I'd heard it from white kids (and one Asian kid) in DC. But I generally ignored the threat of these occurrences. I must have either dismissed the harm or believed my proximity to whiteness protected me, which speaks either to my privilege or my delusion (probably both).

My family rarely discussed race, so it was on my own as a teen that I started to wake up to race and racism. I began to consider the dynamics of race and power around me and throughout the world. I witnessed the rising anti-apartheid movement, I watched every episode of the *Eyes on the Prize* series, I started to choose race-related topics for school projects, and I began developing a deeper understanding of how I was perceived as a young Black woman. My last year in high school we moved to Southeast DC, and for the first time since we left Ethiopia, I lived in a majority-Black area. I became more intimate with the disparities I usually drove by or through on the way to white spaces. I witnessed my discomfort when I passed public housing on my walk to the Metro. I contended with my perceptions about race toward various people and theirs of me. A white acquaintance from my private school expressed hesitation about coming to our new neighborhood, and I felt hurt. I ached to understand what Blackness meant in the world and in me and this investigation just happened to coincide with my initial exploration of Asian spirituality.

My brother, Asgede, I can thank for this introduction. I was sixteen when he left home to live in the local Hare Krishna temple. The preceding year, he dove into ancient Asian teachings and pulled me in with him. He gave me *Siddhartha* by Hermann Hesse. He showed me the I Ching. We both adopted vegetarianism. After he became a full devotee, I absorbed all I could from him and his saffron-robed friends. I went to *kirtan* (call-and-response chanting sessions) at the O Street temple in DuPont Circle and, alongside the white hardcore kids who came for the free meals, I listened to lectures on the Bhagavad Gita and the Upanishads. On my own, I began chanting, tried meditating, and burned a lot of incense. I also became interested in the occult (hence the palm reading) and read about past lives and ghosts. My poor immigrant parents were distraught about what in the hell was happening to their children, but I was resonating with the deeper possibilities opening up for me. For the first time, I had spiritual practices in which to take refuge—albeit in random and mostly misguided ways—from my confusions, disappointments, and fears. Senior year, when my first boyfriend dumped me after only three months of dating (if you can call awkward hanging out and my mostly avoiding him "dating"), I chanted HARE KRISHNA on my mala beads to soothe the pain.

As a teen starting to shape my own worldview, I never really turned to consumerism as the answer to my challenges. This was partly because my father was a Marxist-influenced scholar and primarily because I did not fit the dominant media images of the time. I could never look like what was being sold out there, so I sought other answers.

Also, I could tell that mainstream society was bananas. Washington, DC, was the murder capital of the world in the eighties. The most powerful people on the planet lived in the city and there was a homeless encampment literally across the street from the White House. I was waking up to the obvious racial underpinnings of inequality at the same time I was understanding the moral failures of revolutionary movements around the world. After a friend of his was killed by a letter bomb in South Africa, my dad explained to me that both the apartheid government and the African National Congress killed people in their homes this way.

Secular life everywhere was clearly a hot mess of hypocrisy. And I didn't have a lot of opinions about religious life because I didn't know it. We had completely lost the religious culture that is the bedrock of Ethiopian society. Due to my father's political activities, we couldn't visit Ethiopia after we emigrated, so I wasn't aware of all that was spiritually absent in my life. I did not have a direct experience of our churches, religious rituals, or deep spiritual practices. I knew that Ethiopia, which was never colonized, is a cradle of an ancient form of Christianity and that it became a Christian nation long before most of Europe. I was proud of that fact. But I could not have imagined the magnitude of encountering a culture steeped in spiritual depth—not until years later when I finally visited Ethiopia and felt it myself. I witnessed the profound faith of people who invoked the sacred in every conversation and smelled the holy frankincense lingering in living rooms. I heard prayers broadcast through church speakers reaching those gathered outside at all hours of the day and night. As a young person, I had not experienced this depth of faith as sights, smells, and sounds. Without access to the religion of my own ancestry, as a teen I embraced Asian teachings and practices in my longing for meaning and search for solace.

During my second year at McGill, I decided to major in religious studies and focus on Hinduism and Buddhism. I did not yet know that the Religious Studies Department at McGill, like many universities at the time, approached Buddhism from an analytical framework wherein religions are studied not as living traditions to be experienced but as history and concepts to be understood. My ignorance about this methodology was not only understandable because I was a naive teenager but also because my introduction to religious studies began in the Anthropology Department with an anthropology of religion class. In that course (the main reason I chose my major), we explored spiritual traditions from around the world, studied the nuances of belief and ritual, and examined the multitude of ways people embody religious life. We must have also read religious texts, but I remember only the images: people from diverse cultures in ritual dance with sacred objects, bodies in communion and celebration, movement and what seemed to me like meaning. Through anthropology, religion felt like a living, visceral process with innumerable manifestations. Something stirred in me that semester, and though all academic disciplines are problematic in one way or another, sometimes I think I should have studied anthropology.

Being a weirdo Habesha (Ethiopian/Eritrean) kid in the seventies and eighties was like working as a tiny, untrained anthropologist of mainstream American culture. Some immigrants stay ensconced inside their own cultural enclaves. Some immigrants assimilate to the greatest extent possible. We did neither. We did not abandon our culture entirely; my parents mostly spoke Amharic at home (although I spoke to them in English), we ate injera regularly, and we were expected to maintain certain norms like showing full respect to our elders and strong generosity toward all. But we also let go of many of our traditional foundations (add "not Habesha enough" to my list); we did not go to church, we didn't listen to traditional music (mostly because my parents didn't listen to music), we didn't attend any cultural or heritage groups, and I did not have Habesha friends aside from a few cousins who were equally Americanized.

Also, I'm a Gen Xer and experienced some of my generation's free-range norms: I was a latchkey kid raised on a steady diet of network TV and its whitewashed/race-neutral perspective. Like most of my generation, I absorbed irony, ennui, and dread like they were oxygen. But I was also extremely sensitive. I could see Reagan was a total fraud (and I was only ten), but I also recoiled when a neighbor kid cheered after he was shot. By the time I entered college, I was desperate for less hypocrisy and more integrity. I went into religious studies drawn to understand different ways of being human, of being spiritual.

THE COLONIZATION OF ASIAN RELIGIONS

Scholars have argued for decades that so-called "religion" is a modern, Western concept that probably has little significance historically or cross-culturally. In many parts of the world, European colonization superimposed a Western Christian model of religion onto differing beliefs, often declaring uniformity of meaning on a multiplicity of practices. We see this clearly with how the concept of Hinduism was shaped by colonization. In the country that became known as India, the British encountered various cultural practices across regions, languages, and time and labeled it one thing. By adding "ism" to *Hindu* (a word used to refer to people around the Indus Valley), the word *Hinduism* was coined by the British to denote the texts and teachings of high-caste Brahmans. The scholar S. N. Balagangadhara argues that "Hinduism" is a falsely unifying label largely constructed by Europeans who privileged written texts over oral forms.[2] Colonization perpetuated this preference for unified sacred scriptures (like the European Bible) over diverse and complex, lived realities. And what about Buddhism? Some people point out that the Buddha was not a Buddhist. Though we call it one thing, the various forms of Buddhism that exist today probably resulted from numerous vernaculars and diverse interpretations that all emerged over many centuries and great distances from the early oral teachings. And like most spiritual traditions interpreted by academics, Buddhism has been defined and shaped by a Western gaze.

The first Western translation of a Sanskrit text, the Bhagavad Gita, appeared in 1785. Translations of South Asian texts into European languages influenced Ralph Waldo Emerson and other transcendentalists (including Walt Whitman) and began the process of popularizing Western interpretations of Eastern spirituality. The Theosophical Society, a group dedicated to the study of religion, philosophy, and science (calling this "theosophy"), formed in 1875 by Helena Blavatsky, continued this spread. Blavatsky posited that *mahatmas*, or "the Masters of Ancient Wisdom," guided her and human evolution as a whole. Though theosophy claimed to be a universal connector of global humanity "without distinction of race, creed, sex, caste, or colour," all these so-called masters were said to come from Asia.

These early Western attitudes toward Eastern spirituality can still be felt today. My friend Sam, who is white, grew up in South Africa within an anthroposophical Christian tradition that draws upon Eastern texts. Anthroposophy is a spiritual and social movement, founded by the Austrian philosopher Rudolf Steiner (1861-1925), with roots in theosophy. When Sam was young, he often punctuated descriptions of his religious upbringing by emphasizing the Eastern influences in his denomination. Somehow, he had absorbed that it was cooler to have that association rather than being "simply Christian." When he told me that, I recognized the alluring story of "the East"—the romanticized ways in which Eastern spirituality has been presented throughout my life. My current relationship to Buddhism is not separate from how "the Orient" was formed in the Western imagination.

Orientalism, a term coined by the late cultural critic Edward Said, describes the longstanding Western practice of perpetuating specific ideas about "the East," namely, exoticizing and patronizing tropes that serve an imperialist agenda. Orientalism is not predicated only on negative stereotypes; there can be great admiration (but also fetishization) in its gaze. Said did not denounce Western scholarship as a whole, but he elucidated how Western scholars depicted the East as being bizarre, backward, and ultimately in need of Western enlightenment. There has been much postmodern critique of the ideas central to the European Enlightenment project, especially its universalist assumptions of objectivity, reason, progress, and truth. Said borrowed the term power/knowledge from the French philosopher Michel Foucault to describe the ways Western depictions of other cultures were used to rationalize domination. Foucault argued that knowledge is always bound up with power and academic disciplines are regimes of power. To know something is to make it an object to control. Power was always underneath the intellectual explorations of Europeans because colonization was always a brutal and violent force that included armies as well as artists, traders, and scientists. Land, people, resources, and culture were all acquirable, and acquisition was the goal. Napoleon Bonaparte's invasion of Egypt in 1798 employed over one hundred experts and intellectuals, including some professional Orientalists. In line with its elevation of rational intellectualism, the colonization project privileged written languages (associated with elite "classes") over oral traditions. In

South Asia, the project of translating ancient texts fed into the colonialist process of domination. Scholarly interpretations of texts produced Orientalist (often simplified) versions of what was in fact a complex interplay of lived practices.

ORIENTALISM AND
WESTERN-CONVERT BUDDHISM

The European study and "translation" of Buddhism has never been separate from the subjugation of its original lands and peoples, the domination of its knowledge, and the exoticization of its culture. Recently, I've started to ask myself how I have participated in the Orientalization of Buddhism as something more exotic, cooler, and more profound than Western religion (Masters of Ancient Wisdom indeed). I am inevitably caught up in the modern dynamic to adopt, acquire, and appropriate. Can I, as a Black person, also fall prey to Orientalism? Is it appropriation only if white people do it?

It's interesting to me to witness older white teachers authentically investigate their relationship to race in America. In a few Buddhist-convert communities, some white teachers are looking honestly at ways the power and privilege of race influences their daily lives. But they never seem to interrogate how Orientalism affected their adoption of Buddhism. I have never heard a white teacher talk about their time in Asia or spending time with Asian teachers in terms of their whiteness or approach the question "As Western converts, do we Orientalize Buddhism?" Western-convert Buddhism is often a mishmash of teachings and cherry-picked practices that present as authentic interpretations of the dharma (the teachings of the Buddha). In convert communities in the United States, teachers (whether Asian-born or not) have cultivated a landscape of mostly white Buddhism that looks very different from its origins, often without questioning how and why it was adopted in the first place and how and why it was changed. Of course, there is also deep sincerity of practice within convert communities (and within me).

One of the primary teachings I have understood from the dharma is not to be in contention with reality. This is a core teaching for liberation. Suffering (*dukkha*) comes from wanting things to be other than what they are. The nature of reality is to be constantly changing (*anicca*, or impermanence) and inherently without a permanent identity (*anatta*, or Not Self). Having contention with how things are involves a fundamental misunderstanding. To want things to be other than what they are is to not understand that every situation has innumerable causes and conditions leading to it and therefore could not be otherwise (*kamma*, cause and effect). The only way not to be in contention is by seeing things exactly as they are. But what if we don't see things as they are but only as we've been taught to see them? Then we can be *unconsciously* in contention with things as they are. An American Buddhist teacher, Joseph Goldstein, tells a story of his Indian teacher, Munindra-ji, who described his Western students as extremely diligent practitioners who were like people fiercely rowing boats, not realizing they were still tied to the dock. I've often wondered, "What is the unconscious rope tying Western students to the dock?" It's likely a twine made up various strands. I think one of the thickest strands is probably whiteness. And you cannot understand whiteness if you don't understand Blackness.

In the first season of Donald Glover's award-winning television series *Atlanta*, there's an episode about a talk show on the fictional Black American Network (BAN). A contentious interview takes place between a rapper and a trans activist about Caitlyn Jenner. Although the rapper, Paper Boi, has caused an uproar after a transphobic Twitter rant, he contends that he has nothing against transgender people and eventually he and the activist come to some understanding of the fluidity and self-determination of gender identity. The interview devolves into absurdity when another guest, Antoine Smalls, joins the conversation. Smalls is a dark-skinned Black teen in Georgia who happens to believe he is a thirty-five-year-old white man from Colorado. Antoine is "transracial" (does not align with the race designated to him), and also happens to be homo/transphobic.

The episode pushes the boundaries of the conversation about identity, pointing to the discomfort of challenging the construct of race in the same ways we challenge the construct of gender. We know race is a construct, an invention of racism. Race was created to justify imperialism and the slave trade. Blackness is not intrinsic in anyone. Blackness is definitely not monolithic.

Yet, Blackness—entwined with the enslavement of Africans, colonization of the continent, and the subjugation of a massive diaspora—has become an indelible concept.

All the country borders in Africa were demarcated by colonization, often arbitrarily dividing one ethnic group between two (or more) countries or aligning people who were otherwise not connected by language or culture. The imagined border between my parents' two "countries" (Ethiopia and Eritrea) is a vestige of brutal Italian invasions. Where the colonizers were defeated remained Ethiopia; where they succeeded became Eritrea. The entirety of sub-Saharan Africa—approximately one billion people, thousands of ethnic groups, and over fifteen hundred languages—this multitude of people is called one thing: Black. My dad's cousin Issaye tells a story of when his family was living in Nigeria, where he was working as an engineer. As speakers of Tigrinya (a language of northern Ethiopia and Eritrea), he, his wife, and children had all learned English by the time his monolingual, rural parents came to visit them for their first trip outside of Eritrea. On their second day there, Issaye's mother became very sick. His father nervously paced the hallways at the local hospital while they waited hours for news. Frustrated by the amount of time it was taking, he finally wandered off—a non–English speaking (nor Igbo-speaking nor Yoruba-speaking nor . . .) old man in search of information. He came back deeply disturbed and said to his son, "These *farangi* are so stupid. None of them speak Tigrinya." He used the same word, *farangi*, that is used for white people.

Language and ethnicity among the African diaspora create deep divides that Blackness attempts to close. For example, I do not speak Tigrinya. I speak my mother's language, Amharic (very badly). Though the two languages have the same root, they're not intelligible to each other. When my parents got engaged, there was grumbling from some people on both sides of the family. They didn't go as far as considering each other farangi, but my parents were perceived as marrying outsiders. Amhara (Ethiopian) feudalists had dominated Eritrea since the 1880s, imposing their language and culture, and a decades-long civil war between the two countries killed over a quarter of a million people. Even within my own family, our Blackness did not align us. Of course, most people of African descent *do* align with Blackness as a shared reality because being racialized through white supremacy eventually links us all. But for many years, you could not explain this alignment to some members of my extended family who, like a number of Ethiopians in the sixties and seventies, insisted they were not Black. Other Africans and, of course, African Americans were Black—not us (although, according to them, we weren't white or Arab or anything else either, so go figure). That kind of complete rejection of Blackness is extreme. And extremely problematic. Yet, I understand how racism teaches you to turn away from yourself. I did it for years. Turning toward myself required study and practice.

BLACKNESS, BUDDHISM, AND TURNING TOWARD MYSELF

In 2016, while traveling in South Africa with a majority-Black group of dharma leaders, I had a long chat with one of our tour guides who was a former freedom fighter in the anti-apartheid movement. Under the apartheid system, he was considered colored (his family originated from India). He explained to me that he identified as Black in solidarity with native South Africans as a member of the Black Consciousness Movement (BCM). BCM attacked the white values supporting apartheid (the Dutch word for "separate"), which included creating hierarchal racial categories, with Blackness always at the bottom. BCM is comparable to the Black Power movement of the sixties and seventies, which also emphasized that freedom would not come through political change alone but it required the psychological transformation of Black people to recognize the innate value of their Blackness. Influenced by the West Indian philosopher and psychiatrist Frantz Fanon and led by Steve Biko and others, BCM insisted that Black liberation depended on psychological liberation from whiteness.

The hierarchization of race has always depended on Blackness as the absolute counter to whiteness. Remnants of the racial order can still be seen across the world where European colonizers forced the movement of peoples between colonies and fomented divisions between various people of color. An intermediary racial rank (often Asian but sometimes an exploited local ethnic group) was used to carry out the colonialist agenda (sometimes violently) through the enforcement of Europeans and often at the expense of Black people. We can still see remnants of these classifications in places like East Africa, where Indian people amassed power and wealth through privileged (but still subservient) relationships with colonizers. Often these groups adopted anti-Black attitudes in the process. An example that is known to many Black people (but less so the general public) is that of Mohandas (Mahatma) Gandhi. When he was living in South Africa as a young lawyer, his stance on anti-Black racism was well-defined and expressed: he believed Indians and whites to be part of an Aryan brotherhood and inherently superior to Black people, which was not an uncommon stance of Indians living there at the time. I did not know this in high school when I wrote a term paper on Gandhi, whose activism appealed to me in my search for nonviolent responses to injustice. I had yet to recognize the profound anti-Blackness coursing through the global culture at large, coursing through me.

Sometimes I wonder why my brother and I were drawn to Asian teachings. We both had been searching for meaning and rootedness, the depths of which were lost when we emigrated. Why didn't we look to our own community, to other Black spiritual traditions? Was my turning toward Buddhism a turning away from Blackness? Of course, this is not a yes or no question. Unlike my aunt who insisted she (and we) were not Black, I am not light-skinned. She could have easily passed as white (or at least not Black), and maybe she did sometimes—like many seeking privilege and respite from the relentlessness of racism, some of whom disappeared into whiteness forever. When I walked down the street in Montreal or contended with neighborhood bullies, I could never *not* be seen as Black. And unlike fictional, "transracial" Antoine Smalls, no dark-skinned, obviously Black person can opt out of being Black and choose suddenly to identify as white. I could not turn away completely from myself. Pastor Michael McBride, a Black minister and activist from San Francisco, uses the brilliant phrase "reaching for whiteness." I did indeed turn toward whiteness when I was younger. Maybe the question is how I used Buddhism to turn away from Blackness. I may have turned to Buddhism because it somehow felt exotic or fit higher in the colonialist hierarchy. But to focus on the turning away keeps me caught in the racist construct. Perhaps the question should be this: How have Blackness and Buddhism taught me to turn toward myself?

Toni Morrison's famous statement that racism is a distraction is one I return to often:

> The function, the very serious function of racism is distraction. It keeps you from doing your work. It keeps you explaining, over and over again, your reason for being. Somebody says you have no language and you spend twenty years proving that you do. Somebody says your head isn't shaped properly so you have scientists working on the fact that it is. Somebody says you have no art, so you dredge that up. Somebody says you have no kingdoms, so you dredge that up. None of this is necessary. There will always be one more thing.[3]

I turned toward Buddhism and Blackness at the same time. I am forever grateful for that synchronicity. I read the books of the

American Zen teacher Charlotte Joko Beck and the Vietnamese Buddhist teacher Thich Nhat Hanh. I began to sit with a Buddhist community. Rather than run from one sense pleasure to another to try and escape the pain of my life, I began to turn toward myself. To meet the confusion and despair directly, I had to face the grief of not knowing my ancestral culture, see the ways I internalized racism, and choose changing my consciousness. As I began to turn back to my Blackness, it was Buddhism that helped me embrace what I had rejected. I read the work of Black feminists like Toni Morrison, Audre Lorde, bell hooks. I devoured *This Bridge Called My Back*, a collection of essays edited by Cherríe Moraga and Gloria Anzaldua, feminist authors. They helped me see clearly the self-rejection I perpetrated when I reached for white culture. Black music and arts began to fill my ears, eyes, and body with a different consciousness. Having never danced much in my life, for me, movement became one way into what Lorde calls "the erotic as power." Erotic referring not to the sexual (only) but to a life lived through the senses. She says:

> For once we begin to feel deeply all the aspects of our lives, we begin to demand from ourselves and from our life-pursuits that they feel in accordance with that joy which we know ourselves to be capable of. Our erotic knowledge empowers us, becomes a lens through which we scrutinize all aspects of our existence, forcing us to evaluate those aspects honestly in terms of their relative meaning within our lives.[4]

Buddhism, too, taught me to embrace every part of myself. That's what the dharma invites—a turning toward the truth of this body. Not often framed in terms of the erotic (the patriarchal saga of world religions is for another volume), the dharma nonetheless also asks us to be in direct relationship with our sensory experience for the sake of freedom and joy. When the conditioning of the culture is cleared away, when I'm not in contention with any part of my being, I encounter a deep self-love awaiting me. Only then am I able to embrace all that I am, which is all that I have been all along.

I used to judge myself for being disconnected from my own Ethiopian heritage. Now I see how my longing for meaning was stirred by my discontent. That dis-ease sparked a search that led to Buddhism and Blackness. I have been turning toward myself ever since, finding a spaciousness that allows for all the parts of me to exist. Some years ago, on a meditation retreat, an image of a tumbleweed came to me. Broken from its roots, it was light and surrounded by the wind enveloping it, appearing like space moving through space. It rolled along picking up experiences of cultural debris and detritus, accumulating and losing and accumulating again. I understood that I was like a tumbleweed, my sense of self an accrual of sensations, memories, thoughts, opinions, stories, and values. All through life, I've picked up what was around me as the winds of life moved me along. Now, I allow myself to roll gently, let go of what burdens my path, and dance lightly across the expanse.

· 4 ·

BELONGING

LAMA DAWA TARCHIN PHILLIPS

WE CAME TO AN abrupt halt. No one spoke a word, not even a whisper. We simply inched up to the edge of our seats. Hovering...

You could hear a pin drop. There was no sound but the soft swaying of grass in the wind and the slow, exhilarated breathing of the members of our small group.

We watched as the giant, ash-gray bull elephant slowly stepped onto our path—gentle, unwavering, majestic. Mid-stride, he turned, at ease, confident, calm, and looked right at us, assessing our presence. Then, he marched past us and continued on his way into the open plains of the Ngorongoro.

What had just happened? Not outside of our Jeep where this beautiful animal had crossed our path, but inside of me? What had just happened inside my body and mind? I had been reset, reconnected by recognition. The powerful encounter with nature shoved me into a realization of what it meant to *belong*—completely.

INSIGNIFICANCE

For most of my life, I had felt insignificant. Like many Americans, my parents were immigrants. Born thousands of miles apart, one in the Republic of Trinidad and Tobago and the other in Germany, they met in New York City in the 1960s where they'd immigrated to escape their respective provincial and unsatisfactory home situations. They came to find freedom in the promised opportunities and prosperity of the United States. The promise extended to those souls courageous enough to abandon the plights of their homelands and to leap into the New World.

Witnessing the struggles of the Civil Rights movement, the assassinations of JFK, Robert Kennedy, and Dr. Martin Luther King Jr. had broken my parents' young hearts and they wrangled with the deep and unresolved divide and tensions in our nation. They asked themselves hard questions about their sense of personal safety and belonging, and whether they could truly thrive as a multiracial couple with biracial children in an era of bias and racial polarization.

I was born to my parents in the summer of 1970. I was about a year old when they left New York City and took me with them. Departing Manhattan Island by boat, we traveled for three weeks, finally settling in Germany to be closer to my German grandparents who offered familiarity and financial support to my parents and their young family.

It may sound strange, but for me, a native, big-city infant, leaving New York City was heartrending and traumatic and it left me with a sense of dread, insignificance and displacement. Unable to articulate my own wishes and needs, I fell into a sense of oblivion and disempowerment. Even before I was able to walk, talk, or understand, I had lost my center and my own sense of belonging.

During childhood, I struggled for many years, trying to find myself by trying to fit in. But like so many people, I felt like an outsider and a misfit. Never quite finding a place I could call home or connecting with people that totally felt like my tribe or kin, I never fully sensed that I belonged anywhere or with anyone, but I neither knew nor understood the reasons why. I kept questioning who I was, why I was here, where I came from, where I was going, and why that had any significance. But, on some level, I knew those questions mattered and I had to find out.

My early traumatic displacement, quest, and the rigorous process of inquiry it sparked later informed my life as a Buddhist monk and practitioner and marked nearly two-thirds of my life. I came to find the unmistaken spiritual answers to these questions within myself over time. But even then, with regard to this material world—our world, not the realm of spirit or the awakening mind—I still felt like the oddball.

Now, standing in an open Jeep in the middle of the vast, African wilderness, I reclaimed myself, my life, and my place in the world—in silence. I reintegrated all the dismembered parts of myself, of humanity, and of the Earth.

And I healed.

I reconnected to the planet as my material source and re-arose as my natural, authentic, majestic true self—in ways both profoundly spiritual and physical. The event changed the course of my spiritual practice and work.

LIFE AS A MONK

I have a confession to make: I love Jesus. As a child, ever since I had heard of the works of the Christ, he seemed like a palpable daily presence in my life; a loving, clear, peaceful, and accepting influence; a teacher.

But when I came to Buddhism at the age of twenty-one, the familiarity with the ancient Eastern practice was instant and I told my friends, "I guess I was always a Buddhist, but I didn't know it."

The process of listening, reflecting, and meditating came naturally, but I struggled with doubts when it came to the more unusual practices of the Vajrayana path like full-body prostrations, elaborate visualizations, unending mantra recitations, and their effectiveness for a modern-day Western skeptic like me.

At twenty-six, after five years of daily meditation practice and soul-searching about where I wanted to go with this path as taught by the Buddha, I entered a Buddhist monastery in central France, where I stayed for twelve years. Seven of those years included back-to-back three-year retreats where I practiced deep meditation. Afterward, my teachers asked me to travel as widely as I could and to teach the dharma to as many people as possible. Consequently, I have been teaching and working as a spiritual guide and Buddhist *lama* (a title for a teacher of the dharma in Tibetan Buddhism) for the last eighteen years, visited over thirty countries, and taught people from over one hundred countries.

Some of the best advice I ever received on the topic of doubt was from another Western teacher and elder who told me, "When you experience doubt, you practice until you overcome your doubt, and then you help others overcome their doubt." That is exactly what I did, and it has proven to be sage advice. It has not only freed me from the mental plague of spiritual self-doubt, but it has also allowed me to guide thousands of practitioners toward a more doubt-free practice and authentic path.

AMPUTATED SELF

In 2018, a group of thirty senior dharma teachers (all of whom were of African descent) met at the Union Theological Seminary in New York's Upper West Side (incidentally, near where I was born, Columbia Presbyterian Hospital). We had all been invited to connect and to share our experiences and spiritual paths as practitioners and teachers. More specifically, we met to explore what it meant to teach Buddhist wisdom as a person of African descent and what it meant to support and to be supported by other teachers of African descent in this emerging community.

As we discussed our experiences and particularly how our experiences were similar to or different from each other's or those of many of our Caucasian students, I came to realize what I call today "the amputated self." (Now, those Buddhists who shrug at the word "self" here, bear with me.)

As human beings who have *not* done the work of reintegrating the many different expressions of our human family or species— the different faces, races, and creeds—we are striding through this planet like the walking wounded. We are amputated from many parts of ourselves that we lost somewhere along the way of our mental, emotional, spiritual, and physical displacement. We are ambivalent as to whether we should seek to love and to reintegrate with what we lost or to hate what we're missing. The fact that we are amputated and in pain causes us to lash out. And since many people are either unconscious of this or feel unable to reconnect to the missing parts of themselves, we find comfort in the hatred we share for all the amputated parts, leaving us feeling incomplete, disfigured, imbalanced, disabled, and broken.

When we are disconnected from our own personal stories as full human beings, we are living in an amputated state. And we can feel it. You can feel it. I can feel it. It feels off, it feels rudderless, and it hurts. The fate of the human amputee is to wander this earth without a sense of wholeness or a true and deep sense of connection and belonging. When we are separated from ourselves and from all the pieces that make up the whole human being, there is only the ongoing search. And since it is impossible to reattach ourselves to our sought-after wholeness outwardly—unless we embark on the inner journey of healing and reconnection from within—we are simply trapped in the feelings of separation and brokenness and we deeply miss our own sense of belonging, whether we are aware or not.

The inner signs of this amputated state are isolation, meaninglessness, loneliness, and depression. The outer signs are hatred, division, and violence. We all know what it feels like to carry hatred inside. You do and I do too. Especially among minorities, anger and hatred related to the wounding of the amputated state are common. The amputated state reflects itself in a lack of human dignity, worthiness and deservedness, and as minorities, we often struggle with the anger and hatred born out of a state of perceived victimhood and disempowerment.

But the amputated state is just as present in majorities and in people who choose to identify with being so-called privileged. Assuming an identity of privilege can be a telling sign that a person is suffering from the same sense of separation. A person in touch with their wholeness, connection, and integration would feel no need for privilege and would not bear the unawareness associated with it.

The experience of perpetration belongs to the amputated state just as much as victimization does. When they play a role in the amputation, "over-privileged" people are just as out of touch with themselves as "under-privileged" people. The anger, hatred and self- righteousness are as loud and rampant in the hearts of the overclass as they are in the psyches of the underclass.

Therefore, I have made it part of my work to practice for the healing of this amputated state and to live that healing within myself. It is a practice to release labels; each day that I sit and hold space for the healing of my own amputation, my body reconnects itself to all mankind ever so slightly more than the previous day. I feel a little less isolated and I deepen my sense of belonging and grace.

Grace has become an important word for me on the path of awakening. It is that sense of having something bestowed upon you for which you have no sense of privilege, but rather a deep sense of humble gratitude and a desire to pass on the blessing. Not idealistically—after all, I am a business leader as well as a spiritual leader—but with the realistic expectation that if I am ready to change my relationship with myself, with all humanity, and with this planet, I am embarking on a relationship for which humanity and the planet have been holding out for far too long. There is no excuse to prolong the separation. I am here; you are here; we are human beings; that is who we are.

What does it provoke in you to reflect on your relationship with your own humanity? Does it make you feel excited or dreadful to consider that this journey to the core of yourself is one of healing your amputations? Does it make you want to reconnect to your missing limbs, knowing that those parts may have a different skin color from your own or may still be holding encoded memories of a species at war with itself and divided over language, ideology, and race?

If you were to call all your amputated parts home, slowly starting the frightening process of reconnecting to the body of humanity in all its shapes, sizes, colors and forms, could you drop your anger and hatred? Could you let yourself be transformed by the recognition of your own belonging?

BIRTH OF A PILGRIM

When I first began my journey to reintegrate my sense of belonging in relationship to our planet, I was sitting under a tree at the Omega Institute in Upstate New York. I had just facilitated a panel discussion on climate for several hundred senior dharma teachers from around the world and the session had left me disturbed, quiet, and pensive. I wondered why, even in a group as conscious and sincerely dedicated to the betterment of humanity as ours, I had felt such hopelessness and discouragement triggered by our discussion. Somehow, it all seemed so pointless, like we were all part of a group of lost children unable to figure out how to get home after dark.

Is that who we are as humans?

While sitting under the tree, I felt the slight summer breeze brush my face and allowed it to guide my inquiry into my own sense of apathy, sloth, and amnesia around my relationship with our planet, and I came to some understanding: My relationship with the planet was asleep and atrophied. Like an amputee, I, too, was walking this earth without any sense of genuine connection to the planet and to humanity as my own body, and without any real intimacy or love for where I was physically.

I decided then that I would not truly be able to be a voice of change in the struggle for justice or a sustainable future if I did not first take care of my relationship with our planet. I looked at what made me and billions of other people turn a blind eye and take our planet for granted. I was like a child with a strong sense of entitlement to a parent's generosity, unwilling or unable to see the big picture, to grow up, to step up, and to enter into a new chapter of love, connection, and responsibility. I decided to change and to become accountable right then and there.

For me, changing a relationship means spending time to deepen my sense of appreciation and understanding for who someone is beyond my preconceived notions and biases. Intimacy is a journey of discovery into the close proximity of another's presence, into the inner dimension of their heart and being, until a new sense of who they are (and have always been) emerges clearer for me to see and feel.

I decided to venture deeper into the heartbeat of the world and humanity to transform my view and my relationship with myself, humankind, and the planet. I knew I first had to do my own growing-up work if I were to have any credible influence on another's important relationship with themselves, humanity, or our planet.

A mother once asked Gandhi what she should tell her son who was eating too much sugar. "Go home and come back in two weeks," he said. When they returned, Gandhi told the boy, "You should stop eating sugar. It is not good for your health." When the woman questioned him about his prior response, he said, "Because at that time I was myself still eating sugar."

I knew that to understand not only what I could do but also what I needed to do in my relationship to this looming global crisis, I had to reexamine my relationship with our planet, up close and personal.

Later that year, while sitting in meditation my intuition told me to travel to the Kingdom of Bhutan. It had been a dream of mine for some time to go and visit.

Since I had been a student of the Indian teacher Padmasambhava for many years, I was delighted to lead a two-week group pilgrimage through Bhutan. Padmasambhava had taught dharma in Bhutan during the eighth century, and many treasured ancient and modern teachings are attributed to him. I visited many of the special sites that he had visited and many of the special caves he had meditated in. Once there, our group was blessed by Bhutan's pristine nature and the love and hospitality of its people.

The time in Bhutan was magical, and there is much to share about our time there that must wait to be the subject of another writing at another time. Of great significance was what occurred at the end of our journey when I sat in meditation in the high mountains, enjoying the view of lush greenery, mountain springs, and the vast valley from my hotel room.

During that meditation, my intuition told me that my next pilgrimage would not be about Buddhism or any other one specific religion or culture for that matter. My next pilgrimage would be a journey specifically to deepen my relationship with humanity as a whole and with planet Earth. It all became very clear: If I wanted to transform my relationship with our planet, I would have to become interested in who and what this planet is, what its needs are, and what it has to offer. To help, I had to understand our planet's heartbeat and its voice. Not only did I have to form a new relationship with Earth, as I had discovered earlier, but I also had to become an actual pilgrim of the planet.

When the idea first arose to lead a global pilgrimage, I thought people might think me foolish for considering such a long and risky undertaking. But inside, I felt an incredible sense of joy with the idea of expressing awareness and appreciation for our planet by traveling around it, by doing a circumambulation of it, and by honoring it in all its diversity and abundance.

The Awakened World Global Pilgrimage—the first ever public pilgrimage around the planet—was born.

It is my hope that the Awakened World Global Pilgrimage becomes a movement. It has that purity and potential. I hope it helps many people transform their relationships with themselves, with humanity, and with our planet and helps people transition from being separated, amputated, and distant to being up close, intimate, and personal.

If you feel inspired after reading my thoughts here, think about how you can make your relationship with our planet and with our species much more alive, intimate, and personal. I believe we will act differently when we have a better understanding of what our relationships to humanity and this planet personally mean to us and how much we have received and are receiving from them every day.

As a person of mixed African descent, I have learned there are wounds in the human psyche that make us seek our sense of belonging by identifying with a small subset of the human race where we feel a greater sense of significance. I call these "the wounds of insignificance." Whenever I experienced separation or abandonment in my childhood, whenever I felt overlooked or disregarded, these experiences exacerbated the wounds.

Nothing drives the point of insignificance home stronger than enslavement. When you lose your status as an equal among your fellow human beings, you experience the wound of insignificance. We must be aware that, by refusing to value people or to dignify their humanity, we are perpetuating the wounds of insignificance and the many distortions of the search for meaning and significance that spring from them. Some of the wounds' most bizarre perversions rise from the seeking of fame and fortune without any contribution to humanity or the willingness to cause harm to others through terror and violence to gain the notoriety we desperately crave.

I have been fortunate not to have been born a slave. And to my parents' credit, being reared in Europe allowed me a degree of distance during my formative years to the traumata of our over-racialized American society and its ongoing culture of mistrust between the majority and minorities.

My childhood wounds of insignificance belong to a different category. They happened quietly while I was growing up abroad, far away from the streets of New York City.

But like you, I know what it feels like to be injured by unconscious family habits, cultural biases, misguided rituals, and traditions. And I know what it feels like to be trapped in a cycle of searching for significance, without first healing the wounds by which the cycle started.

COLORLESS

As a person of mixed African descent, I know there are many experiences that could make someone feel insignificant. And I feel for those people who have internalized or accepted those fallacies inflicted upon them as truth. For me, these experiences and the subsequent limiting beliefs that stemmed from them are not true even in the slightest. Or, I should say not true any longer.

Today, I do not feel insignificant because I do not *make* myself feel insignificant, no matter what is happening in my life.

But I understand we live in a world in which deep wounds of insignificance have given rise to distorted versions of success, where some people feel the need to suppress and exploit others, win at all costs, or stash away lifetimes of assets to inflate a false sense of self while suffering from feelings of inconsequentiality.

In the United States, we have a lot of work to do to communicate to our children that they are significant because of *who they are* and not because of *where they rank* in the hierarchy of things. A distorted sense of significance seeks recognition, fame and the accolades of achievement, not from the perspective of mastering a craft but for the sake of outperforming others and coming in first. Being the "most," "biggest," "fastest," et cetera, is associated with being more significant. The virus of our insignificance has seduced us into dysfunction and has alienated us from ourselves.

As a practitioner of dharma and a teacher of mixed African descent, however, I feel quite differently about our true identity: I believe that the liberated mind has no color at all. I believe that in our heart of hearts, we are neither black nor brown, neither yellow nor white, nor pink or any other color. In our liberated mind, we are free; we are beyond color.

I am saying this because it is important for us to experience ourselves in both dimensions: the dimension of the fully integrated person who can connect completely to all colors and cultures while recognizing that none of the colors and cultures truly do us justice in our true essence (beyond color or creed), and the dimension of being simply human, as we present ourselves in our natural habitats, embodied as black, brown, or any shade at all. As spiritual beings, we must realize that we are beyond color, that at no time does the color of our skin hold any sway over us. What controls us are our wounds of insignificance.

Some of these wounds have been perpetuated by centuries of slavery and colonialism; some of these wounds have been perpetuated by social incompetence, interpersonal ignorance and confusion. Whatever their origin, we must learn to identify and to honor a colorless, liberated heart and mind just as much as our fully embodied, beautiful, black, brown, and white bodies, and heal the trauma of our lack of safety and lack of significance.

The promise of the dharma is universal liberation for all, regardless of origin, race, gender, religion, or sexual orientation. One of the reasons dharma appeals to so many minorities is its focus on liberation from struggle, pain, and suffering.

But, on the path to greater liberation, one challenging part comes in allowing yourself to release your identification with your color and race. I am not suggesting that it is not deeply important and meaningful to own our ethnic heritage or to heal all the shame and resistance to fully inhabiting ourselves. It is both critical and essential. But we also want to dismantle the oppression of being identified with our history of suffering from trauma and insignificance so we can recognize our timeless value in knowing the true identity of our colorless nature, which is eternally liberated and always magnificent.

As dharma teachers, we share the message that inside each and every one us, there lies the flawless, colorless nature of awareness and liberation. If we do not share this message, we do all our brothers and sisters a disservice— repeating the injury of reducing us to the color of our skin and restricting their vision of their own liberation.

When we manage to enroll someone in a vision of their own healing and liberation, it becomes more interesting to heal the present than to heal the past, and it becomes more interesting to acknowledge wholeness than to become holy. Waking up is a discovery process of who we already are, not a search for who we can become. No less is what we must accomplish if we want to heal the demons of our past with regard to race in this world.

I have traveled the globe and I have seen wholeness and dignity in all corners of the world. Everywhere, you can find totality and healing, regardless of a person's socioeconomic state or social position. We are carrying a burden of wounds that have not healed and identities that have not been allowed to re-signify themselves from a ground of colorlessness, soulfulness, and wholeness.

How can we have these kinds of conversations about healing when so many people are still walking around amputated from the rest of their own humanity? How can we speak about forgiveness or complete reconciliation when the pain of our own amputation is still tormenting our minds and the wounds are still fresh?

Do we even want healing? Do we even want reconciliation?

Do we want to belong to each other, to our species, to this world? Or would we prefer to stay alienated and irritated enough to care that things aren't solved, but not exasperated enough to solve them once and for all?

When I embarked on the path of dharma, I thirsted for liberation, not for rehabilitation. I wanted freedom more than I wanted name and stature. And the price for that freedom was no less than everything.

"Everything" meant surrendering the sense of belonging to one group of people over belonging to all humanity. I had to abandon my sense of insignificance (according to history) and accept the confidence and significance of being fully present.

You cannot remain a black person and realize the meaning of dharma. You cannot remain a white person and awaken to the full potential of your true nature. You cannot elevate one gender over another and receive the most precious gift this world has to offer. You are either all in, or you remain a prisoner confined to the walls of your own making.

The Buddhist master Thich Nhat Hanh once said in his poem "Call Me by My True Names":

I am the mayfly metamorphosing on the surface of the
    river, and I am the bird which, when spring comes,
    arrives in time
to eat the mayfly.
I am the frog swimming happily in the clear pond,

and I am also the grass-snake who, approaching in
  silence, feeds itself on the frog.
I am the child in Uganda, all skin and bones,
my legs as thin as bamboo sticks,
and I am the arms merchant, selling deadly weapons to
  Uganda.[1]

To evolve oneself through the practice of wisdom and compassion means to declare one's willingness to outgrow not only
the suffering in our genes but also the causes of the suffering.
To become truly human thus calls for us to renounce all amputations, regardless of the underlying bias and experience that
caused them.

It is deep and vulnerable work and there are no shortcuts.
You cannot simply wish your wounds away. An amputated
heart and mind do not reconcile through further separation but
through the realization of nonduality and the full reintegration
of all aspects of itself.

Can we be courageous enough to admit to ourselves the experience of amputation? Can we be courageous enough to admit to ourselves the existence of our wounds of insignificance
and belonging? Can we be courageous enough to venture on a
journey of rediscovering and redeveloping the relationship with
ourselves, with humanity, and with the planet, until we experience those relationships as ones of love, respect, significance,
and belonging?

Can we overcome the experience of being a tourist in this
life, entitled to taking whatever we want from our experience and
leaving only trash behind, and instead transform into pilgrims
on a sacred journey, traveling in life to reconnect with all our amputated parts until our sense of wholeness is fully restored? Can
we step into all of who we are, fully embodied, and discover our
colorless, liberated self-less being that is ever powerful, gentle,
and unharmed as if we had arrived on the very first, timeless day?

My practice and work are committed to the deep healing
within myself and to the people who choose to trust me to guide

them. To me, that is a great honor, because in supporting the healing of just one of us, we are learning to heal us all.

CONCLUSION

I fell into my seat inside the Jeep. No one spoke a word. It was as if there was no more to say, as if any word uttered now would simply taint the recognition that had occurred inside of us, among us. No one wanted to leave behind the deep sense of oneness, wholeness, and belonging that calmed our hearts and minds with the elixir of truth. In silence, we drove off slowly into the evening sun.

While we watched the elephants, zebras, wildebeests, lions, cheetahs, and rhinos in our rearview mirror disappear, we were hopeful about our new direction, which was no direction at all. We set a course all of us could finally arrive at: a view and path that held the potential to offer healing and restitution in the deepest sense. Restitution would not come in the form of assigning blame or responsibility, or of living in the shadow and pain of our amputation. No, restitution would arrive in the greatest form of all—being fully restored to our rightful place in the world and to the majesty of our true belonging.

That is an idea worth spreading.

· 5 ·

VOLUNTARY SEGREGATION

The Paradox, Promise, and
Peril of People of Color Sanghas

PAMELA AYO YETUNDE

I AM A PERSON OF African descent. I grew up in a lower-middle-class black family and neighborhood and attended a predominantly black United Methodist Church (led by a white pastor during most of my youth) in Indianapolis, Indiana, in the 1960s and 1970s. I grew up believing that to secure God's salvation from eternal hell, I had to attend church weekly and commit to at least one type of service to the church. Having learned to fear God's punishment, I became a member of the church youth group and eventually became a leader in that all-black youth fellowship—my first segregated spiritual community.

My middle and high school years in Indianapolis took place during a racially tumultuous time when black public school students were being integrated into white-populated public schools through court-sanctioned bussing, nearly two decades after the United States Supreme Court case *Brown versus Board of Education of Topeka* was decided in 1954. I became aware some white people believed black-populated schools were intellectually inferior to white-populated schools, and by way of implication, black people were innately intellectually inferior to white people. Why didn't I know this sooner? Fortunately, my parents did not make what white people thought about black people apparent to their children. I grew up in a black neighborhood and rarely dwelled in white spaces. As a young child, my world was de facto, and to an extent, voluntarily segregated by race.

In 1972, when I was eleven years old, I was bussed the first time and I was fifteen years old when I was bussed the second time. The first time, our bus was met by an angry mob of white adults. The second time, a student-led race riot occurred at another high school, putting us on notice that violence could erupt at our school; violence did not erupt because our high school had an armed security guard to provide a silent and steady uniformed brand of specific deterrence. Entering high school was the first time I experienced being policed. It would have been easier and safer (perhaps) to stay in a predominantly black school, but because bussing was court-ordered and because my family was of limited means (my parents could not afford a private or parochial school), my neighbors and I were bussed away from my neighborhood school, just five blocks from our home, twice before it eventually closed down. It closed because white people were not bussed to our school. Even if more black families with young children had moved into our neighborhood, the children would have been bussed to white schools. Indeed, staying in one's place when others have to leave is a privilege, but privilege is not the same as power. And even though white people were in a position of privilege and power, white families opposed to racial integration could not permanently prevent our court-ordered arrival.

Closed schools depreciated home values in our neighborhood. Depreciated home values negatively impacted the community. For example, the public library within walking distance of the school and where I spent my childhood eventually closed and became a church. Our public park and pool, named after Wes Montgomery (the famous black jazz guitarist from Indianapolis), hosted a youth tennis program founded by Arthur Ashe (a black tennis star and Civil Rights activist). Some of my fondest memories of growing up in Naptown were spent playing tennis at "my" black park, where I played hours upon hours of tennis with my Arthur Ashe graphite racket. That was Black Power to me! Over time, the tennis courts were removed and the pool became a small water park. The neighborhood, many decades later, has not recovered from bussing.

Looking back on these formative, identity-making years, I see how much destruction of my community was set in motion by bussing, and at the same time, I am led to wonder if racially integrated public school education actually prepared me for resilient living in a racially pluralistic country. Though it was not the intent of *Brown v. Topeka Board of Education* to promote psychological resilience through racial integration, I cannot help but wonder if that was one of its unintended consequences for people like me. I now ask, What was the formative and developmental impact of my all-black United Methodist youth group involvement while I was bussed the first time, and did these parallel experiences psychologically prepare me for being bussed the second time? Do racially integrated spirituality groups, in this case sanghas (Buddhist practice communities), promote psychological resiliency and liberation for black people? In this chapter, I intend to reflect on my experiences with encountering the dharma (Buddhist teachings) in white-populated sanghas, my initial ambivalence about participating in POC (people of color) sanghas, the invitation to form a POC sangha, and helping form and teach in POC sanghas. Lastly, I will share the insights I have gleaned from those experiences.

ENCOUNTERING AND PRACTICING BUDDHISM IN INTEGRATED SANGHAS

Like many African American people, I grew up in the United Methodist Church. I had two maternal great-uncles who were United Methodist pastors, and their sister (my adoptive grandmother) and my mother followed in that tradition. I first encountered the core of Zen Buddhism (though I didn't know it at the time) in 1999 when my work colleague—we were stock traders—gave me a copy of Stephen Mitchell's translation of the Tao Te

Ching. When I finished reading this short text, I felt a peace I had never felt before. I was amazed! Reading the Tao Te Ching was not like anything I had ever experienced from reading a spiritual text. In 2001, a month after the World Trade Center bombings, a friend gave me Thich Nhat Hanh's *Touching Peace*, and right around the same time, my hospice volunteer application was accepted by Zen Hospice Project in San Francisco. Reading the Tao Te Ching and *Touching Peace* and entering into Zen Hospice Project as a volunteer—all around the same time in the course of my spiritual maturation—opened my eyes to nondualism, mindfulness, and the process of confronting existential angst. All this took place in predominately white-populated communities.

When the idea of forming POC sanghas was first brought to my attention at a meditation retreat for POC led by Nhat Hanh, I was firmly against the notion of racially segregated spiritual communities. The POC retreat was attended by approximately five hundred people, including my sangha friend James, a person of Filipino descent. My opposition was a result of my previous life-altering experiences at Zen Hospice Project and Community of Mindful Living sanghas, but I was willing to consider the invitation to explore the idea more.

James and I decided we would discuss the idea within our small, mostly white sangha, and when we brought it up, the suggestion just to talk about the notion of POC sanghas was met with thick, impenetrable resistance. This resistance, which came especially strong through a particular white-bodied man in the group, was of an intensity I had not experienced in many years, maybe not since I was eleven when our school bus was met by an angry white mob. It was his resistance which led me to believe that forming a POC sangha might actually be a good idea. But, I didn't pursue it at that time because I felt that sitting in silent meditation with white people was a fortifying experience to prepare for facing white people "off the cushion," in real life when we aren't in meditation—without fear, without self-loathing or other-loathing, and without internalized apartheid (a subject I return to later).

With the exception of that one instance of resistance, the

whole of my experiences with white sanghas had been affirming—but that was in the San Francisco Bay Area in the early 2000s. My subsequent experiences in two sanghas in Atlanta proved to be another story in contemporary racism, demonstrating to me the need for POC sanghas.

When I was living in Atlanta, I had become a Community Dharma Leader (CDL), a lay Buddhist leader in the Insight Meditation tradition (a westernized Theravadin Buddhism). When I entered into the Insight sangha in Atlanta, I was welcomed by some but I was also met with harsh criticism by others for speaking dharma, as if I had no authority to do so. In fact, I had authority granted by Spirit Rock Meditation Center (the organization that leads CDL trainings), but that authority isn't enforceable (not that I would want to enforce it) and not recognized by many. My speaking up eventually caused such a disturbance for two white men that they trolled me on our Buddhist list serve! In a subsequent planning meeting, one of the trollers screamed at me at the top of his lungs because I asserted myself as a confident Buddhist teacher. Eventually, the sangha disbanded over a financial rift, but it was no place for a person of color to speak, lead, or be perceived as leading.

Even after the experiences with the resistant white male in the Bay Area and the two white men who trolled me in Atlanta, I started the Sacred Refuge Sangha (SRS) in Decatur, Georgia, and I made it open to all because I still believed POC sanghas were not the ideal community for me to spend my limited spiritual practice time in.

As the founding leader of SRS, I was responsible for many things including giving dharma talks and organizing space for others to do so. When I gave my first dharma talk (a talk that was scheduled for only fifteen minutes, on the topic of equanimity), a white woman during the question and answer period criticized my talk and proceeded to give her own talk. I reached out to her afterward and learned that she wanted to become a dharma teacher. So I invited her to give a talk, and she accepted. After her talk, she told me that she appreciated how not everything that can be said on a topic can be said in fifteen minutes. She also told me she was self-conscious the entire time and realized she was not ready to be a dharma teacher. I thought we had come to an understanding. When I gave another dharma talk on another evening, this same person, after hugging me, patted me on top of my head! I interpreted this behavior as an act of condescension and a breach of physical space. When this happened, it built upon my experience of thick resistance in the Bay Area, the trolling behavior in the other Atlanta sangha, and the woman's previous attempts to discredit and diminish me as a Buddhist leader. The case was now built for me to start engaging in POC sanghas, but I still decided not to start another sangha.

After two years of weekly leadership, I closed SRS because no one was willing to take the lead. The "business" of holding a sangha, POC or not, requires regular attention and care from at least one handful of people, and as it grows, two handfuls and more. Eventually, another sangha started with a new leader and new name, but with one of the same unapologetic trollers. It was not a safe place for me, so I decided not to join. I was glad to be free of the leadership role as well as free from the community itself. I was free to explore being a part of another sangha in Atlanta, where I had met some lovely and impressively rebellious white Zen practitioners.

This new Zen group shared leadership among its members and had a zeal for community education. They offered a multipart series on how to offer dharma talks and they opened their workshops to the public. The series was led by a white Christian theology professor. (I never learned why they asked a non-Buddhist to lead these workshops.) Just before the series ended, the organizers asked if there were other topics they could offer workshops on. Since I was someone who had worked as a chaplain and pastoral counselor, someone who was in a doctoral program in pastoral care, and someone who had written on Buddhist spiritual care, I offered the topic of "Buddhist pastoral care." The idea was embraced with enthusiasm. When the organizers asked who could teach it, I offered myself. Again, there was positive curiosity. We scheduled a meeting where I told them about my education and experiences, and no concern was expressed.

Months later, one of the organizers asked me if I was going to *attend* the workshops on Buddhist spiritual care—the same workshop topic I had proposed that I could lead months earlier. I told her that I hadn't heard about it, and when I asked who was leading it, she told me it was a white male Christian pastor—the husband of the Christian pastor who led the previous workshop. At first, I was stunned, but it wasn't long before I felt rage, and I respectfully let her and others in the room know I was enraged. I was met with silence by some, confusion by others, embarrassment by a couple, and one white man said out loud that he really didn't care how I felt.

To be invisibilized was painful. To express anger and rage in a Buddhist community was risky. To be met with indifference in a community that preaches compassion? Unconscionable. Yet, through the power of anger and rage, I gave a very compelling dharma talk on the cost of being attached to one's passions, even if they are noble.

Even after all my other experiences in sangha race relations, I still felt some resistance to creating POC sanghas, so even this was not the final straw to break the proverbial camel's back. I asked myself, in good Zen fashion, *What can I learn about myself through this?* and in good *lojong* (a Tibetan Buddhist compassion practice) fashion, *What is the unpredictable thing I can do now?*

Rather than leave this sangha, as an act of compassion for myself, I did the unexpected. I decided to stay where I felt unwelcome by some. I stayed several months. Owing to what I had learned about Buddhism and Zen from the various readings I had done, the experiences I had in the sanghas I had joined and started, and the trainings I had been part of, I found the confidence to stay.

One of the things I learned by staying was that those who were prone to treat me as if I were invisible, incompetent, or unworthy of empathy also didn't treat some other white people with respect. I also realized something about my own resilience by staying in a group of white people I had lost respect and trust in. I discovered I wasn't dependent on them to teach me Zen, but I sat with them to understand something about myself. I found I could practice the dharma in a community that I was not dependent on for teachings, and I saw that I was learning less and less from this community. These realizations had implications for my off-the-cushion life as well, a subject I return to later. I left and vowed not to be a part of an all-white sangha in Atlanta, ever again.

BEGINNING TO PRACTICE IN POC SANGHAS

Sometime after leaving the sangha to continue my years-long practice of sitting at home exclusively, I decided to venture into Shambhala (a westernized form of Tibetan Buddhism). I was interested to check out this sangha because I had benefited greatly from reading the books written by a Shambhala nun, Pema Chödrön. I attended one of her retreats about a classic Buddhist text entitled *The Way of the Bodhisattva*.

At the Shambhala center in Atlanta, I went to a talk by Dr. Gaylon Ferguson, an African American Shambhala dharma teacher and professor at Naropa University (and the author of this book's foreword), and he espoused the creation of a POC sangha at Shambhala. There were many African-descended people in the room—more than I had ever seen in the Community of Mindful Living, Insight, or Zen sanghas I had attended. I could hear Dr. Ferguson in a way I had been unable to hear Dr. Larry Ward, an African American dharma teacher in the Community of Mindful Living, the first time I received the invitation to create POC sanghas. My mindset was now different and my environment was different. This time, I was in a room full of African-descended dharma practitioners. The combination of my experiences and Dr. Ferguson's talk in that room let me see the possibilities of a dharma community that could address the particular needs of POC. In other words, in my mind, the idea went from abstract to concrete.

Months later, after I finished my doctoral dissertation on the psychospiritual lives of African American Buddhist lesbians using the black feminist poet-essayist Audre Lorde's writings on the importance of self-preservation, I made a presentation at the Parliament of the World's Religions about Lorde's spiritual development.[1] Thereafter, it occurred to me that there might be people at Shambhala in Atlanta who would like to know about Lorde's spiritual journey and how her experiences illustrated the spiritual developmental of a bodhisattva (someone who puts the awakening of others before their own), even though Lorde was not a Buddhist. I contacted Shambhala, and an African American woman named Bev invited me to give the presentation. Sometime later, I was invited by another African American woman, April, to give a dharma talk to the newly forming POC sangha. I titled the talk "Conversations with People of Color: Cultivating Your Bodhisattva Self." The description read,

> The purpose of this three-part series for people of color at Shambhala is to explore what it may mean to cultivate a bodhisattva self in a "racially suspect" body, in an increasingly dangerous US context. In part one, we will discuss our views on *The Way of the Bodhisattva* by Shantideva, followed by an examination of Black lesbian poet and activist Audre Lorde's spiritual journey, followed up with a conversation on cultivating the next steps in our own bodhisattva paths.

After offering this three-part series, I was asked to offer another series titled "To Be Beautiful, Colorful, and Buddha-ful: Building an Inclusive Practice Community for Confident Living." My friend, dharma teacher, and Community Dharma Leader, La Sarmiento (who founded Insight Meditation of Washington (D.C.) POC and LGBTQ groups in 2006) was the inspiration for the word "Buddha-ful," which they sang in a song they wrote to One Direction's "What Makes You Beautiful" melody. In this series, I touched on the following themes:

Sitting Together So We Can Stand Together
Practicing for the Welfare of Others
Living with the Experience of Being "Othered" and
    Lovingkindness Meditation
Nonviolent and Compassionate Responses

The Paradox of Safety and Insecurity
Cultivating Joy in the Midst of Sorrows

If you are contemplating starting a sangha for POC, I recommend these themes for your consideration and planning.

Sitting Together So We Can Stand Together

In many Buddhist traditions, people engage in sitting meditation. Why? It is said that the Buddha achieved enlightenment through sitting meditation. What does enlightenment mean? In short, the secular explanation is that Siddhartha Gautama (the historical Buddha's name) became liberated from the delusion that he could transcend the vicissitudes of life. The spiritual explanations for the Buddha's enlightenment include liberation from extreme views, liberation from death, liberation from greed, hatred, and delusion, and liberation from false notions of self, material matter, and separation. By sitting together, POC may experience a variety of forms of secular and spiritual liberation; to be liberated in any of these forms promotes the ability to be in solidarity with others.

Practicing for the Welfare of Others

In the Buddhisms I am most familiar with (Community of Mindful Living, Insight, Soto Zen, and Shambhala), people enter practice to ease their suffering. But if they stay with the practice and study, they will soon come to know that the ultimate motivation for practice is so we become benefactors; we donate the fruits of our practices so that others may be free. There are Buddhist teachings and practices called "dedication of the merit." Dedication of the merit is setting the intention that any practice benefits (merit) be offered to others. This is a radical practice in letting go of a precious experience so that others can be released from suffering. In a relational sense, this means carrying the precious experience as a gift so that when others encounter us, they are not harmed but rather nourished and even possibly liberated. In spiritual and secular senses, this dedication promotes radical generosity as we work to transform the delusion of separation. As Martin Luther King Jr., influenced by the same Hindu teachings—*ahimsa*, or the practice of nonviolence, and Indra's net, or the interconnectedness of everything—that helped give rise to Buddhism, said in his "I Have A Dream" speech:

> But there is something that I must say to my people, who stand on the warm threshold which leads into the palace of justice: in the process of gaining our rightful place, we must not be guilty of wrongful deeds. Let us not seek to satisfy our thirst for freedom by drinking from the cup of bitterness and hatred. We must forever conduct our struggle on the high plane of dignity and discipline. We must not allow our creative protest to degenerate into physical violence. Again and again, we must rise to the majestic heights of meeting physical force with soul force. The marvelous new militancy which has engulfed the Negro community must not lead us to a distrust of all white people, for many of our white brothers, as evidenced by their presence here today, have come to realize that their destiny is tied up with our destiny, and they have come to realize that their freedom is inextricably bound to our freedom. We cannot walk alone.[2]

Paradoxically, transforming the delusion of separation may also need to happen in a POC sangha when divisions arise over ethnicity, culture, gender identification, sexuality, religion, political views, roles, and responsibilities.

Living with the Experience of Being "Othered" and Applying Lovingkindness Meditation

When I think about my sangha experiences in the Bay Area and in Atlanta, and when I reflect on conversations I have had with many POC dharma practitioners in different places, I realize what we want to talk about in our voluntary segregation is our experiences of being "othered." In this context, I am using the word "othered" to mean being experienced as less than an ideal human being. POC need healing containers to talk about these lifetimes of repeated experiences without encountering opposition as we do so. Touching on these subjects can give POC rise to negative surprises, anger, rage, feelings of betrayal, being overcautious, seeking permission to be authentic, and having a concern about retribution. In other words, sharing publicly about such oppressive experiences is likely to fuel the sense of a separate self if it is not met with welcome and understanding. POC talk about being "othered" in many places, but typically not in contexts where we also talk about lovingkindness meditation in the same breath—no pun intended.

When practiced thoroughly and regularly, lovingkindness meditation is an antidote to anger, hatred, rage, and separateness. In essence, lovingkindness meditation is a practice that involves sitting, practicing mindfulness, and visualization. What is being visualized, generally in sequence and for predetermined amounts of time, is one's self, someone else who is loved, someone for whom there is no love or hate (neutral feelings), someone for whom there are intense negative feelings, and then there are visualizations of being at home and throughout various realms in the universe. Each phase of the visualization is met with an attempt to feel love. Lovingkindness meditation is not to be used as an escape from real feelings that are not akin to love but are used as a method for transformation over time. The wisdom in having a lovingkindness meditation practice is the knowledge that othering is a part of the human condition and knowing we have choices about how we are going to practice resiliency in the face of persistent ignorance.

Nonviolent and Compassionate Responses

There are a variety of ways to respond to a culture that doesn't always celebrate POC. One might say that POC don't need mainstream American culture to celebrate us, or that there are holidays and parades that celebrate the cultures of POC, but I would argue that we are still pieces of the dream and not yet permanently stitched into the patchwork of the US multicultural and multiracial quilt. In the meantime, how do we contribute to a culture in such a way that we do not make it more violent than it already is? Refrain from reacting violently to violence—how do we do that? The Buddhisms I am aware of espouse radical nonviolence. Take this excerpt from the Kakacupama Sutta (a story about the Buddha in the Theravadin tradition), "The Simile of the Saw," which is from the collection of suttas (sermons) in the Majjhima Nikaya, or in English, the Middle Length Discourses of the Buddha:

> Bhikkhus [monks], even if bandits were to sever you savagely limb by limb with a two-handled saw, he who gave rise to a mind of hate towards them would not be carrying out my teachings. Herein, bhikkhus, you should train thus: 'Our minds will remain unaffected, and we shall utter no evil words; we shall abide compassionate for their welfare, with a mind of lovingkindness, without inner hate. We shall abide pervading them with a mind imbued with lovingkindness; and starting with them, we shall abide pervading the all-encompassing world with a mind imbued with lovingkindness, abundant, exalted, immeasurable, without hostility and without ill will.' That is how you should train, bhikkhus.[3]

This *sutta* reminds me of words attributed to Jesus while he was dying at the hands of his persecutors. According to the Bible in the book of Luke, 23:34–44, Jesus said about his persecutors:

> Father, forgive them, for they know not what they do.
> Then Jesus said to a criminal being persecuted with
>   him who wanted salvation:
> Truly, I say to you, today you will be with me in
>   paradise.
> And just before he took his last breath, he said:
> Father, into your hands I commit my spirit.[4]

The Buddha and Jesus taught that embodying radical loving-kindness, even in the midst of being violated, is the ultimate way.

I don't share this sutta to say that self-preservation is unimportant; despite what some of the Buddhisms teach, I believe self-preservation in the face of annihilation is a moral act of rehumanization. Self-preservation does not require hatred of the attacker but love enough of the self—especially for POC trying to survive various, often intersectional, forms of race-based violence. But we can imagine having the capacity to remind people, in the moment of them hurting us psychologically and emotionally, that they still have the capacity to do better and that eventually we are willing to be a vehicle for their transformation. Why do I write "eventually"? One has to have the motivation to change. So it may be futile, even a bit violent, to force positive change on someone who is vehemently against the suggestion.

The Paradox of Safety and Insecurity

We want a sense of safety, but we know deep down, we are insecure. We come to POC sanghas with a desire to feel safe from the negative gazes of white people, hostility, invisibilization, and lack of empathy—but we still remain insecure and conflicts still arise. For example, there was a disagreement between two African American women in the nascent Shambhala POC sangha in Atlanta, leading one of them to leave.

Do we feed the delusion of safety by coming together in POC sanghas? Do we exacerbate our insecurity outside of sanghas when we do not deal with insecurity inside sanghas? Must we deal with insecurity to get to safety, and does dealing with safety exacerbate the reality of insecurity? I think it is important for POC sanghas to teach their members how to practice equanimity by accepting safety as a desire, aspiration, and fantasy, while also accepting insecurity as a natural part of being human. Through acceptance of our desires and our nature, hopefully we can be relieved of suffering insecurity as a site for shame to manifest and fester, and thus minimize the potential for shame to be unconsciously projected onto others.

Cultivating Joy in the Midst of Sorrows

In popular culture, Buddhism is often talked about as the religion that focuses on suffering and compassion. For POC sanghas, it is important that space be made for the recognition and expression of the sorrow of living in racist societies. Simultaneously, space should be made for the cultivation of joy. Theravadin and Insight traditions commonly highlight the teaching of the Brahma Viharas, or the heavenly abodes. Lovingkindness is one of those abodes; another is sympathetic joy, or the feeling and expression of joy for another's feelings and expressions of joy. But what about our own joy? I believe joy for one's own experiences is necessary for the whole of Buddhist practice so long as the joy is not self-aggrandizing, competitive, an attempt to be pleasing, or contrived to mask authentic negative feelings. POC sanghas should allow for humor, laughter, fun, and delight in addition to contemplation, because off the cushion, we may not have space for expressing radical joy. In fact, in some Buddhisms, it is taught that this much joy may be so addictive that it can pose challenges to finding liberation through contemplation. I have not found that to be true for everyone. How do we proceed to create containers for liberation?

I believe these basic themes may be helpful to consider and discuss when starting a POC sangha. How the sangha continues (and actually how it begins) will be up to the community, but if the sangha founder(s) and leader(s) do not know where to begin, I suggest using these themes as starting points.

NAVIGATING CHOICES SURROUNDING POC SANGHAS AND AFFINITY GROUPS

After my journey with the Insight, Soto Zen, and Shambhala sanghas in California and Georgia, I moved to the Twin Cities of Minnesota (Minneapolis–St. Paul) in 2017 to teach at a liberal Christian seminary. Shortly after I arrived, I was invited to meet leaders in the Insight community and the Soto Zen community.

Both communities have POC leaders, POC affinity groups, and POC retreats. The POC and non-POC people I met were hospitable, and I went on to give dharma talks to the wider communities as well as the POC communities. Well-regarded African American dharma teachers, trainers, and authors Rev. angel Kyodo williams and Ruth King visited to facilitate exploration of how interracial Buddhist sanghas can be welcoming and can contribute to improving communications, healing, and fostering solidarity in our Twin Cities Buddhist communities. Their work is inspiring. And, I have personally benefited from the efforts people in the Twin Cities POC sanghas and white ally sanghas are making to transform their communities. Although these communities, at first glance, seem to offer options for POC, the options are still limited. POC practitioners can attend the all-community (and thus nearly all-white sangha), or they can attend the POC or other affinity group sanghas where white people *may* be encountered, or they can go in and out of sanghas as they feel moved. Considering these options leads me to ask: Are these ways of voluntarily segregating ourselves to work on ourselves uninterrupted by white gazing and animosity to be permanent structures with permanent participants? Permanent or not, what is the purpose of POC sanghas if we are not practicing nondiscrimination ourselves?

SOME ADVICE FOR POC
CONSIDERING ENTERING A SANGHA

For POC who are brand-new to Buddhist sanghas and are entering these sanghas for liberation from the suffering racism inflicts, I recommend first trying to find a POC sangha or affinity group. I suggest this not because I believe all mostly white or all-white sanghas support racism but because a large concentration of whiteness (a collective representation that may be interpreted as hostile) will likely compound the suffering a POC is trying to transform. If there is no POC sangha in your area, start one and consider the themes I mentioned above. If there is a POC sangha, you may find yourself welcome there, but it would be helpful to enter it knowing that there may be disagreement or discord. In other words, go in without the delusion that POC sanghas offer complete safety. Understand that all communities need to figure out what they are going to be and how they are going to operate. The stereotyped fantasy that Buddhism results in the elimination of conflict and that "good" meditating Buddhists are emotionally unperturbed will not be helpful in building and maintaining POC sanghas.

When entering a POC sangha, tell them why you are there and ask them if they will support you in your practice. If the answer is "no," then you will know you are not welcome. If the answer is "we'll try," then give them the chance to meet you where you are. This will require vulnerability, transparency, receptivity, and humility. Why humility? You are entering into a belief system and community you are not familiar with. It will take some time before you come to your own conclusions.

How can you trust that the POC sangha is actually about liberation? If the POC sangha is a community where the practitioners' main motivation is to avoid white people, I do not believe its mission is deeply liberative. In sanghas like these, we may enjoy each other's company, we may sit in silence for a while, we may feel temporarily safe, but we don't talk about our responsibility in transforming our own states of consciousness so that we all operate in the world without the delusion that all white people are evil. Think about Malcolm X, or el-Hajj Malik el-Shabazz, as he was known after his pilgrimage to Mecca. His devotional experiences with white Muslims transformed his state of consciousness. The Zen Buddhist ways of Thich Nhat Hanh and of other teachers in the Zen tradition are not the ways of separation, just the opposite. These schools of the Buddha way are the way of interbeing, interconnection, and interdependence and are thus congruent, in a transcendental sense, with African *ntu* (interdependence) cosmology and spirituality.[5] A POC sangha that does not allow for practices and teachings in interdependence unwittingly supports what I call "internalized apartheid," the often unconscious ways we voluntarily segregate ourselves from white people because we feel weakened, threatened, or inferior in their presence. A liberative Buddhism supports strength, confidence, and equality, or in other words, what I call "Remarkable Relational Resilience"[6] in the face of the negative white gaze, real and perceived. How is this done?

In my dissertation research, I used a combination of a survey and interviews to determine the psychospiritual experience of African American lesbians in the Insight tradition. One of the areas I explored was the tension between the necessity for self-preservation in the face of racist, sexist, and homophobic oppressions and a Buddhist practice and teachings that say there is no self to preserve. What I learned is that these women do not interpret "no self" in the sense that some European-descended Insight dharma teachers and writers have done but in the African spirituality *ntu* sense: "no self" means "no independent self." Their belief in no independent self (stated otherwise as interdependence)—along with a lovingkindness meditation practice, meditation retreats, mindfulness, and participation in sangha life—contributed to Remarkable Relational Resilience in a world that could easily lead these women to live introverted, isolated, self-centered, alienated, and internalized apartheid existences. Contrary to popular opinion about Buddhism only being about aloofness, depending on how Buddhism is understood and practiced, it liberates and heals. And, surprisingly and paradoxically, this healing from oppressive separation may begin in a voluntarily segregated POC community. When I was encountering Buddhism in 2001, championing integrated spiritual spaces, I never would have expected to hold the views I now hold.

INTERNALIZED APARTHEID, LIBERATION, AND THE POSSIBILITY OF A POSTCOLONIAL BUDDHISM

Since I first encountered the heart of Zen Buddhism through reading the Tao Te Ching in the late 1990s, I have practiced in four Buddhist traditions (Community of Mindful Living, Insight Meditation, Soto Zen, and Shambhala) in three states (California, Georgia, and Minnesota). Much has happened during those years. The attack on the World Trade Center on September 11, 2001. The election of Donald Trump in 2016. The brazen white supremacy and nationalism in the White House. Mass internments and deportations of adult immigrants and their children, including asylum seekers. These developments have led me to see how politics, policy, and rhetoric in the United States contributes to the ebb and flow of ease and dis-ease, as well as the need for spiritual practices to ease the intensity of our innate dukkha so that we may contribute to an ever-evolving civil society. POC sanghas can contribute to civility or contribute to internalized apartheid, depending on the sangha's mission.

POC sanghas that consistently raise issues and concerns pertinent to the well-being of their members and consistently share teachings from the way of a dharma-inspired life contribute much to civil society. By contrast, those that do not intentionally foster a liberative mission may actually promote fear, spiritual stagnation, internalized apartheid, and an unproductive "refuge" from the white gaze.

What can make the difference between investing in growth, skillfulness, contemplation, courage, civility, and liberation on one side, and a feel-good get-together in the interest of the dharma, on the other side? Having sat in different POC sanghas, I believe POC sanghas should create a mission statement which expresses that its purpose is to cultivate the liberation of POC. Dharma talks by POC, dharma resources created by POC, dharma practices created by POC, sutta interpretations from the lenses of POC in their cultural contexts, iconographic images of POC—all these offerings honor our creativity and wisdom and acknowledge the realities of our lives.

By supporting dharma practice and expression for POC practitioners, POC sanghas help contribute to a postcolonial Buddhism. They revisit the ways Buddhism has been Westernized to identify and reintegrate back into Buddhism the wisdom of POC, including Asian Buddhist teachings that Westerners have largely discarded. I recall asking a lay Insight Meditation leader if she thought Buddhism was a shamanic tradition, and she immediately scoffed at the notion of the Buddha engaging with spiritual beings in various realms of existence. But if the definition of shamanism includes a belief in entities that exist in realms we cannot see but can communicate with and be empowered by, then how do we explain the following sutta?

> As the Blessed One [the Buddha] reflected thus [on not wanting to teach because of the difficulties in doing so], his mind inclined to living at ease, not to teaching the Dhamma.
>
> Then Brahma [a god or deity] Sahampati, having known with his own mind the reflection in the Blessed One's mind, thought: "Alas, the world is lost! Alas, the world is to perish, in that the mind of the Tathagata, the Arahant, the Perfectly Enlightened One, inclines to living at ease, not to teaching the Dhamma." Then, just as quickly as a strong man might extend his drawn-in arm or draw in his extended arm, Brahma Sahampati disappeared from the brahma world and reappeared before the Blessed One ... Then the Blessed One, having understood Brahma's request, out of compassion for beings surveyed the world with the eye of a Buddha.[7]

Because many Buddhist schools have long histories of offering shamanistic teachings, it's clear that indigenous Buddhism includes shamanism. And since postcolonial spirituality involves excavating indigenous teachings, those wanting to practice a postcolonial Buddhism stand at the threshold of reclaiming the shamanistic side of Buddhist practice. When giving cultural-contextual treatment to the dharma, POC may find themselves tapping into postcolonial ways of knowing, remembering, reintegrating, and broadening realms, worlds, and relations through shamanic worldviewing. A shamanic worldviewing may serve to integrate a mentalized Buddhism with a magical and mythical and mystical Buddhism more akin to our indigenous roots.[8] If POC who are interested in returning to the roots of Buddhism can tolerate indigenousness (we've been taught over the centuries to reject our own ways of knowing), Buddhist POC spaces will be sites of liberation from suffering as well as sites for reconnecting to our indigenous ways of knowing.

How can we proceed on a postcolonial or decolonizing Buddhist path? In brief, on this topic I have been influenced by the writings of Rev. Dr. Emmanuel Y. Lartey, a Ghanaian United Methodist minister, psychotherapist, and professor of pastoral theology. He says that postcolonizing the Western view of the Christian god involves seven aspects: (1) counterhegemonic; (2) strategic; (3) hybrid, as in promoting multidimensional discourses and practices; (4) deeply interactional and intersubjective; (5) dynamic, as in constantly in flux; (6) polyvocal, as in many voices participating; and (7) creative.[9] I believe his method need not be limited to what non-Western Christians must do to be liberated from colonized minds but rather it can inform what POC in colonized Buddhist communities can do to experience wholeness: integrate their traditional, culture-laden worldviews with their Buddhist liberative practices.

BRINGING RIGHT AND WISE INTENTION TO POC SANGHAS

Voluntary segregation, especially by black folks in the twenty-first-century United States, is puzzling to many people. I was saddled with my own resistance to POC sanghas for many years until several race-tainted incidents convinced me otherwise.

I was born into a Christian family. While growing up, no one ever told me I had a choice of religious and spiritual paths. Though my positive encounters with Buddhism were arguably providential, they were also indicative of something more. African Americans do not come to sangha through the force of the intergenerational transmission of slavery, Jim Crow, segregation, and vigilantism, which used Christianity to keep black people in subjugation (even though it was turned back on the oppressors in liberative theologies of resistance). We come to sangha through freedom of choice. For those who freely choose Buddhist sanghas, it is not always clear what exactly is being chosen, but the appeal of quieting the mind (through meditation, chanting, or other devotional practices) is a draw.

The number of African Americans entering sanghas seems to be on the rise. Given the increasing visibility and respectability of POC dharma teachers and leaders, there are more POC sanghas and affinity groups for black folks to enter into without ever having first attended a majority-white sangha. POC sanghas can be refuges from white inhospitality. POC sanghas can promote near-instant vulnerability in sharing our stories with each other, but being in majority-white sanghas can also teach us something.

Knowing your intention when you choose a dharma community is critical to evaluating your experience of that sangha. How can Right Intention—the path factor in the Noble Eightfold Path that says suffering ends, in part, when wholesome desire is cultivated in the mind *before* acting—be brought to choosing a sangha? POC sangha teachers and leaders do well when they take our cultural-existential situation into consideration in crafting and providing talks on topics such as safety and insecurity, building solidarity, cultivating resiliency and joy, and balancing the experience of being othered with practices in lovingkindness and compassion. Leaders and teachers can do so in ways that do not compromise the dharma but give cultural and contextual treatment to the dharma. In this way, as POC listeners hear the dharma, their experience is enriched and made practical through cultural interpretation and application.

POC sanghas are refuges from many things, containers for a variety of experiences, pathways to true community, and places of liberation from isolation and alienation. Healthy POC sanghas promote freedom and resiliency. They can be crucibles for transforming old habits, but more than that, POC sanghas can be places that help us return to who we truly are and have always been—the no self that is undivided, aware, free, confident, compassionate, fearless, empathetic, and responsive.

· 6 ·

FROM BUTCHER TO ZEN PRIEST

Radical Transformation through Bloodletting

GYŌZAN ROYCE ANDREW JOHNSON
WITH PAMELA AYO YETUNDE

Rad·i·cal: (especially of change or action) relating to or affecting the fundamental nature of something; far-reaching or thorough.

Trans·for·ma·tion: a thorough or dramatic change in form or appearance.

THE YEAR WAS 2005. It was one of those ordinary, bone-chilling, dreary, and snowy days in the Midwest, but this would turn out to be no ordinary day in my life. This day was the beginning of my renunciation of butchering dead animals for human consumption and my transformation toward becoming a Zen priest. As the day began, I had no plan to give up my work, had no idea what renunciation was, and didn't know what Zen was, so therefore I had no plan to become a Zen priest. So how did a butcher without a plan to be otherwise become a Zen priest who no longer butchers? I accidentally did to myself what I intentionally did to the animals and experienced my own near-death bloodletting. In the aftermath, I lived among the dying and let die what needed to die in order for me to live. What follows is my Way Seeking Mind story—my way to Zen.

BECOMING A BUTCHER AND DISCOVERING THE MEAT OF MYSELF

I first started in the butcher trade as an employee in a supermarket meat department back in the early 1990s. There was good money to be made in the trade at the time, and I took advantage of the opportunities presented. Through hard work, I earned my way into an apprenticeship position and later became a journeyman meat cutter. Cutting meat occurs long after the actual animal killing, which happens in processing plants and ranches, so I was many degrees removed from killing. In processing plants and some ranches, the animals are cut into subprimals (a piece of meat larger than a steak but smaller than a side of beef) and are then aged and shipped to a market, where butchers do the skilled work of making retail cuts. This is the work I was doing. It begins very early in the morning in a refrigerated room. Speed, accuracy, and volume are all critical aspects of the job, and to do this type of work over the years—in my case, day in and day out for a decade—requires much physical and mental stamina, as well as a mastery of the craft. I became very proficient at my craft.

One spring day in 2005, I was washing dishes in my apartment after returning home from a day of butchering. Of course, I knew how to wash dishes because I had washed countless dishes over the years, but at this particular moment I used too much pressure on a stoneware plate I had propped inside the sink at an angle, and as I washed it, it broke into several pieces. One of those razor-edged pieces sliced with considerable force directly into my wrist. This shard severed my first three tendons—my thumb, index, and middle fingers—and, more dangerously, my radial artery. The radial artery supplies oxygenated blood from the lungs to the arm and hands. I was in serious trouble.

This mundane afternoon of washing dishes became a threat to my life. The blood loss was immediate and weirdly stupendous! The blood flow was immense, gushing with force from my body like water from a firehose. My hand was literally hanging away from my wrist; the meat of myself, like the meat of all the animals I had cut, was exposed for the world to see. The butcher had become the butchered. No separation. How Zen! Each heartbeat (which are finite, I've realized) was literally spilling out through the wound. The cut, the gushing blood, and now the pulse. There was too much to process, and I was overwhelmed. I gasped in shock, which gave way to terror. I was absolutely stunned at how egregiously injured I had become in an instant, simply by washing a plate. In my wildest dreams and nightmares, I had not imagined I would die from careless dishwashing—I am a black man, after all. Nor did I imagine I would die from an accidental cut to myself—I was an experienced butcher, after all.

During my time working as a butcher, I had millions of opportunities to injure myself. Working at high speed and high volume, butchers consider it inevitable that there will be minor lacerations from time to time. But that is while working with bone-cutting band saws, commercial meat grinders, bladed tenderizers, and knives of every manner. So, the irony of a master butcher causing himself a life-threatening wound while washing a plate at home was not lost on me. Later, I wondered if there was a karmic connection between my injury and past activities. What causes and conditions led to a serrated clay blade from a tilted plate cutting through my wrist with the swiftness of a bone-cutting band saw, revealing the meat of me as I had revealed the meat of animals? But there was one critical difference between me and the other meats—I was still alive!

Coming out of shock and terror, I committed to not squandering my life, so I cradled my right arm against by body and raced downstairs to get help from my neighbor. Without the use of my arms, I frantically kicked his door as if I were trying to kick it in. My neighbor angrily threw open the door, wondering out loud what the racket was about. He looked down at my cradled arm, his eyes popped wide open, and he called 911. He didn't invite me in, so as blood continued to pour out of me like water from a fire hydrant, I slumped down against the house to take comfort on the stable ground and curled my body into the fetal position. The cut, the blood, the noticing, the shock, the terror, the arrival at my neighbor's, and him calling 911 all occurred very quickly. I bled profusely for ten minutes without any abatement. After ten minutes of blood rushing like a stream, I become semi-conscious. My vision and hearing began to fade, but I was conscious enough to hear the siren of the ambulance approaching.

WHEN MEAT MEETS MEDITATION: SOUTHFIELD, MICHIGAN—WINTER, 2005

Some months after I accidentally cut myself, I was sitting in the passenger seat of my friend's car while he took me to my first meditation sitting. I don't know why I agreed to go. I hardly knew anything about mindfulness meditation, but I was willing to go despite the fact that I was nervous about it. The closer we got to the meditation center, the more anxious I became. What was I expecting? What was I afraid of?

My nervousness, I believe, stemmed from a near-conscious acknowledgment that I had a lot of mental work to do and that work would require me looking at uncomfortable and unpleasant places of the mind. I knew it needed to be done, but I felt fear about exploring uncharted territory. Luckily, I was also curious enough to work past the nervousness. I had already prepared myself for encountering meditation by voraciously consuming many of my friend's books on Buddhism and Zen, including *Zen Training: Methods and Philosophy* by Katsuki Sekida and *Insight Meditation: The Practice of Freedom* by Joseph Goldstein. I read these books in tandem to find a balance between classic Zen training and working with the feelings and emotions that arise in meditation. Looking back, I see that reading these books contributed to my radical transformation from butcher to Zen priest. What hooked me in these readings was the new understanding that I could finally discover tools, a process, and a practice with a strong physical component. It was like discovering something I knew I needed, but I didn't really know I needed it until I found it. I learned that healing through meditation was as much about the central nervous system as it was about the mind. I understand now that the two are not separate. This understanding gave me an appreciation for Buddhism and Zen before I ever practiced meditation. Even so, when I entered into the meditation space, my anxiety grew.

Something inside of me, like a knowing that I could not put words to, suggested that there is a radical difference between Buddhist philosophy or meditation and Buddhist people. It was the fear of going inward with people who also went inward which gave me that uneasy feeling. In retrospect, I think that what led me to press on in the face of anxiety was the energy of karma (cause and effect), which is imperceptible, beyond linearity and logic, and without beginning or end. Karma, ultimately, led me to meditation.

When we arrived for meditation, I clumsily removed my snowy boots in the small foyer and entered into the warm kitchen. My low-key anxiety attack was exacerbated by what I witnessed there: a half-dozen orange-robed Sri Lankan monks chatting amicably among themselves and a group of lay practitioners. And the attack was further intensified by what I interpreted about them. Ridiculously, because I was in anxiety attack mode, I truly feared these monks could read my mind! Did I read somewhere that monks could read minds? Of course, my rational adult self (when he returned to himself) understood mind-reading to be ludicrous, but this fear came unbidden, and I believed it. After all, if I wasn't ready to really know the contents of my own mind, I certainly did not want others entering into it. But what if they had entered my mind—what would they have found? The unexamined mind of a black butcher!

A LIFE-AND-DEATH CONFRONTATION WITH KARMA

The EMTs assessed that my blood pressure was so dangerously low that I had to have an emergency blood transfusion.

Ten minutes later, at the emergency room, the doctors quickly determined that I needed to undergo surgery. General anesthesia was administered shortly thereafter, but not before they injected me with a useless local pain killer and cinched the blood pressure cuff so tightly that my arm turned dark purple. Although the cut and the bleeding caused me to nearly lose consciousness, I was conscious enough to experience the worst physical pain I had ever felt.

After compressing my arm into a dark purple hue, the doctor pried into my wrist, trying to locate the radial artery to tie it off. I was familiar with prying, having myself pried into countless interstices of the subprimals I made into retail cuts of meat. But that familiarity did not cease the pain. As the prying continued, my mouth produced a steady stream of expletives. I apologized, but the agony continued. What seemed like forever, but was only about ten minutes, resulted in the doctors mercifully intubating and anesthetizing me. But I was told that, even while sedated, I fought the anesthesiologist during intubation. Though I was alive, I was also near dead.

The whole of my injury, seeking care, and receiving treatment planted the seeds for what I sensed that first day I went with my friend to the meditation center: I had much unexamined karma that needed to come to light for examination. My pain and helplessness made accessing unexamined karma of utmost importance.

After a successful surgery, a cast was placed on my right arm starting below the elbow. My body had been treated, but in my mind, I was still living a nightmare. I so badly wanted to go home, sleep, and awaken from the nightmare called my unexamined life. In some way, I felt myself to be waking up, but what exactly was I becoming more aware of?

Because there was no room on the post-operation floor, I was placed on the oncology floor before being released back into the world. Surrounded by cancer patients, I felt as if I were nearly in a charnel ground (a public place where corpses are gathered for cremation ceremonies and rituals). My body was better, but the reality of my own near-death experience was accentuated by being surrounded by dying people. Pain, nightmares, and charnel grounds are also dharma gates (experiences that lead to awakening), and I was walking through them all. As I lay in the oncology ward, another one of the dharma gates I found myself confronting was the reality that I had other people's blood coursing through my veins so that I might live.

Drip by drop, several units of blood were put back into my body. I was also drugged through a morphine drip. Through the drips of blood and morphine, I faded in and out of consciousness. When conscious, I heard the shrieks, moans, and wails of my fellow patients on the oncology floor charnel ground. When I was lucid enough to consider my predicament, I felt fear and disbelief. I asked myself, "How in the actual f—k did this happen?! I gotta go to work tomorrow. How will you pay your bills? What did you do, Royce?! You effed up buddy—big time. You had it comin'. What's going to happen to me?" My thoughts were like raw meat that bled from the near-conscious mind to the forefront. Denial was no longer a defense. Negative narratives and aggressive self-talk flooded my mind and central nervous system. I could not go home to sleep off this nightmare.

The next day, the doctors removed my morphine drip while I had a stunning, to-the-core headache. My throat was raw and abraded from the intubation and my fight while sedated. My abdominal muscles felt as though I had done a thousand crunches. One cut. Lots of blood. The tight cuff. The prying of the wrist. Intubation, morphine and blood. My whole body in pain. The negative self-talk. The cries of oncology patients. One cut and the meat of my life, perhaps of life itself, had been revealed for me to see. Self-pity turned to an appreciation for life when it occurred to me that not everyone walks out of oncology. People die there—and I was alive and would be discharged soon. I did not want to squander my life.

FAMILY, RACISM, AND INTERGENERATIONAL TRAUMA

My father, who is black, grew up in Jim Crow–era Birmingham, Alabama. To escape racist oppression, he joined the army. While stationed in Germany, my father met my mother, who is white and was also eager to escape her circumstances. They married in the 1960s and boldly returned to the United States, where being an interracial married couple was illegal in many states. My parents had three children before migrating to Inkster, Michigan, during the Great Migration, the period from 1916 to 1970 during which approximately six million African Americans fled the South to the industrial North. I was three months old when we moved to Inkster. Inkster was one of the destinations where black people knew they could find high-paying jobs at Ford Motor Company. Its founder, Henry Ford, philanthropically supported the community and its predominantly African American population with several social programs, in addition to the excellent wages they offered. My father would eventually retire from Ford as a comptroller.

My mother became a clinical psychologist, primarily working in the prison system. She often expressed her contempt and disdain for all things religious or spiritual because she had no use for what she deemed uncertain or imaginary. My parents, having seen the evil that people do to one another, in the United States and in Germany, chose not to raise their children with religious beliefs. One of the benefits of being raised without a religion was that, as I entered into Zen, Buddhism, and training for the Zen priesthood, I had no religion to disentangle myself from. I had no doctrines or dogma to abandon. Therefore, I could be inextricably entangled in the buddhadharma. What I didn't know was whether I could be disentangled from intergenerational trauma, the meat cutter karma, or the everyday sufferings of a black man in America. Nevertheless, the year 2005 was pivotal on the path of radical transformation.

LIVING WITHIN PARADOX

The doctors informed me I would need to wear the cast for about twelve weeks to allow for sufficient healing from the intricate surgical reattachment of the tendons and artery. But after about seven weeks, I removed the cast myself because I had determined it was time to go back to work. Because I was unable to use the cast I had destroyed, I fashioned a makeshift rig of various athletic braces. I could put it on for stability and take it off for flexibility, as needed, to continue the physically demanding work of butchering early in the morning in refrigerated rooms.

Why did I return to butchering? Why not? Much of my life was paradoxical. On one side, there was an African American and on the other side, a white German. On one side, there was a fledgling Buddhist leaning into wisdom and compassion. On the other side, there was a butcher on his grind, punching the clock to earn a living in that cut-throat (no pun intended) meat cutter world. Straddling these polarized worlds posed challenges to me as to how I might soften into the reality of my life, and life beyond this world. How could I proceed with my life, in all its contradictions, in the wake of such a traumatic event?

During the time between when I cut myself (spring of 2005) and that winter when I first entered a meditation center, I deeply contemplated what I was reading. The summer was full of reading the writings of Zen masters who asked koans, unanswerable riddles intended to inspire nondiscursiveness to coax students from their fixed views and dualistic thinking. They asked, "Who are you?" "What is this?" "What is your original face before you were born?"

My answers? I didn't have any, but I continued contemplating. I found a picture of myself taken when I was three months old, in 1969. The photograph had yellowed, but I could still see me—the tiny being crawling on the bed and looking up at the camera. I posted the picture on my refrigerator in my apartment to remind myself that I was actually born at one time. In the past, I had been so distracted by life that I had literally forgotten this fact. My life was becoming one of fewer distractions, and, as such, I was not going to forget that being of the nature to be born, I am also of the nature to die. Wearing my cast reminded me. With the photo of my baby self on the refrigerator and the cast on my adult arm, these reminders of being born and of dying brought back memories and stories of intergenerational oppressions and migration.

DISCOVERY AND COMMITMENT ARE THE CHOICEST CUTS: DETROIT, MICHIGAN—WINTER, 2006

In 2005, I worked at a market for economically privileged people in Troy, Michigan. In 2006, I worked for Detroit's only black-owned supermarket. This grocery store served as an oasis in the food desert of Detroit. Before my first day there, while keeping warm in my car in the early morning as I waited to step into yet another cutting-room and join yet another crew, I saw a predawn spectacle: a procession of twenty-one police cars with all their sirens screaming, driving down Grand River Avenue. I later learned they were hunting for the killers who had shot and killed one of their own just minutes before. Watching the caravan of police cars and hearing the sirens reminded me of my vulnerability in the presence of police as a black man in Detroit. I wondered, *How might I move freely in my world and the world at large?*

In about a year's time, I had gone from being an anxious, fearful-of-having-my-mind-read meditator wannabe to a Buddhist practitioner. I was aware of the precepts—the ethical and moral foundation of Buddhism, including nonharming and Right Livelihood. Right Livelihood means not contributing to or receiving the proceeds from work and industries that create harm, cause suffering, or refrain from compassion. In traditional forms of Buddhism, Right Livelihood had been reduced to refraining from industries that produce weapons, traffic human beings, engage in the meat business, trade in intoxicants, or produce poison.

So, here I was—a butcher embarking on a Buddhist path. But I didn't let my profession deter me from learning about Buddhism and Zen. Why? This quest was more about how to survive, not what work was appropriate. The police caravan was in frantic pursuit, and I still wanted to protect myself—the Buddhist-butcher-biracial self—from the fear and realities of police brutality against unarmed black men. How? Staying on the path has produced some insights.

I began reading Zen and Insight Buddhist literature in 2005. In 2006, I found myself on the fence about which Buddhist tradition to undertake, believing I could not or should not deeply pursue both. I chose Zen as my main dharma gate on the Buddhist Eightfold Path to the radical transformation of suffering. Zen is not always the tastiest or the prettiest, but for me it's the best medicine. I had stumbled upon a traditional and serious Korean Rinzai Zen temple in the inner-city community of Hamtramck. Their primary practice is zazen (silent sitting meditation) and koan introspection. Through Korean Rinzai Zen, I continued on the path of radical transformation by letting go of living only "from the neck up." I became reacquainted with the central nervous system and experienced brief, sporadic periods of stillness. I had come a long way from my first meditation experiences, where I was only able to sit for five to ten minutes at a time, to now an hour without fidgeting. I sat with the sangha (Buddhist community), an ever-changing mix of people of varying races, ages, and sexes. Together, we were doing what we believed had to be done—ease our suffering, together.

In 2006, I cobbled together my own Zen practice around my work schedule (cobbling arm casts for my injured wrist was good preparation). When possible, I would spend two or three weeknights at the Zen Center, sitting with the sangha in the morning and evening and being available during the day for Zen Center tasks and projects. As much as I could, I immersed myself in this community, and in return I received the benefit of invaluable Zen training. Often, I would go directly from the Zen Center to my job, from cushion to cutting board, and that transition was surprisingly easy for me. I was amused by the apparent contradiction of it all. After all, paradox and contradiction, black-white-butcher-Buddhist-African American-German is who I am.

From cushion to cutting board and back was my practice for nearly three years. Nearly three years of practice taught me I had become ensnared in the collective mentality of my working-class world, which included the suffering of adolescent male posturing and its vanity, which is accompanied or caused by an underlying sense of lack and scarcity. I had become separated, cut off, and isolated from living an authentic life. I had become like the animal that had been separated from its species, killed in a sense, and thus cut off and cut into pieces. In Buddhism, it is said that greed, hate, and delusion are the roots of much of our suffering. I saw in myself that leaving the roots of suffering to fester can also cause further harm to oneself. This insight led to my commitment to radical self-compassion and radical self-acceptance. In retrospect, this was the kind of protection I was seeking when the caravan of police cars screeched and screamed before me. Zen helped me to be a black man who can also live more equanimously with the threat of police brutality, and still care for myself deeply. As I was learning to care for myself, my sister in Texas reached out to me.

DEEP, DEEPER, AND DEEPEST—EMBEDDING IN THE WORLD OF ZEN: HOUSTON, TEXAS—2008–2009

The year 2008 was the year of the Great Recession. The Great Migration brought my parents to Michigan and the Great Recession would be my reason for leaving. The Big Three automakers (including Ford Motor Company, where my father made a career and a life) were nearly bankrupt and the ripple effect throughout the region was catastrophic. My sister reached out from Texas with an invitation to relocate. So in 2009, I loaded up my salt-rusted Neon and began my singular great migration southwest. I became an economic refugee, fleeing the land of lost economic opportunities. I didn't know if I'd pursue butchering in Texas. All I knew was that in 2009, I would not be able to do in Michigan what my father did in the 1960s.

In March, in Michigan, one tends to stare down the barrel of at least another month of cold, wet, dismal weather—but not in Houston, Texas. Moving from Michigan to Texas in March was like watching a black-and-white movie that suddenly switched to vivid Technicolor. Temperatures were in the low eighties, flowers seemed to bloom everywhere, there was sunshine, and the smell of sweet floral perfume was in the air! I sensed I was in the right place to really heal not just my wrist, my arm, my anxiety, and my angst but also my core sense of separateness. I felt I was in an excellent healing environment, and I really wanted to be healed.

When I left Michigan, even though I had spent a lot of time at the Korean Rinzai Zen Center, I still felt that my practice was tenuous, so I made it a priority to seek out a practice place and a sangha as soon as possible upon arriving in Houston. Initially, I had this grandiose plan of visiting every Zen center and Buddhist temple in the city, but practicalities, proximity, and karma (that which is beyond perception and logic) quickly whittled down the list.

I walked through the gate of Auspicious Cloud Temple (the Houston Zen Center) and into a space bustling with energy as the community engaged in its annual yard sale. I was greeted by a well-comported and collected woman with bright, kind eyes. I noted she possessed some of the outward qualities I had previously observed in other folks with decades of meditation experience: she was gathered, calm, still, and with a receptive openness. This woman was Konjin Gaelyn Godwin Roshi, and she was to become (and still is) my root teacher in the Soto Zen lineage. Choosing this lineage meant committing myself to the Zen teachings that had been transmitted from Shakyamuni Buddha to Shunryu Suzuki Roshi, the founder of the San Francisco Zen Center. I soon become a regular attendee, then a member, then a resident. This was my first experience living within a Zen community full-time, and I took to it with enthusiasm and resolve.

The practice life at Houston Zen Center can be viewed as two parts. On the one hand, there are the day-to-day responsibilities of maintaining the property, such as organizing everyone's activity, shopping for food, and tending to the many details involved with offering retreats, *sesshins* (week-long practice intensives), and workshops. These responsibilities might be considered mundane or as necessary chores to be completed. However, I have come to realize these things are none other than the practice of Zen itself.

On the other hand, alongside the mundane aspect of temple life, there is following the daily meditation schedule, teaching or participating in the many classes that are offered, and taking part in the practice forms and ceremonies that are the heart of our Soto Zen lineage. The folks that comprise the large and thriving sangha that is Houston Zen Center offer themselves with their generosity, morality, energy, patience, meditative stability, and wisdom.

By 2012, I was still employed as a part-time butcher while living at the Zen Center. At work, I was an incognito Buddhist. None of my coworkers were aware that I lived at a Buddhist temple. These mostly white, older, staunchly Christian native Texans did not strike me as being very open-minded or understanding to much outside of their own experiences. To save myself the grief and energy of having to constantly explain and defend myself, I chose to simply omit sharing that part of my life with them.

The ability to set aside the inner chatter (or ignore it), focus on striking a bell at the appropriate time, or offer a meal in a specific way are mindfulness practices; these practices would certainly serve me well in the future. The little seeds of a future Zen priest had been planted and watered, and so the transformation continued. Over the next four years, I continued to live this life of service and practice and eventually I began to wonder if it was time to take yet another leap.

THE BUTCHER BECOMES A PRIEST: SANTA LUCIA MOUNTAINS, CARMEL, CALIFORNIA—SPRING, 2012

My leap landed me in California at Zenshinji, or Tassajara Zen Mountain Center, founded by Shunryu Suzuki Roshi. At Tassajara, the fall and winter seasons are divided into two different ninety-day practice periods. This is a time for formal, dedicated, and deep practice, which can take many forms. Within these practice periods are several concentrated intensives (sesshins). The spring and summer are open to guests to come and enjoy the Japanese hot springs, attend a meditation retreat, and experience the seclusion of the valley. During this time, the monks work in various roles supporting the monastery and the transient community. Throughout my time at Tassajara, I moved through various positions and eventually became one of the temple officers—a senior staff person.

It had been nine years since my first visit to a meditation center, where I had a panic attack and feared the monks could read my mind. So much had happened: I had increased my time on the cushion, become a member of two Zen centers, lived part-time in a Zen center and then become a full-time resident, and been in long-term retreats. I decided yet again to take a leap (it was becoming a habit), and I asked my teacher if she would ordain me as a Zen priest. Wonderfully, she agreed, and I (with the substantial help of many beings) began the process of sewing my priest's robe.

Why does a Zen priest have to sew their own robe? This manual backstitch sewing practice takes patience and commitment. Developing patience and commitment are aspects of cultivating a bodhisattva ethic—putting the enlightenment of others before your own; manual backstitching allows the postulant to thoroughly explore their intention with each stitch. In 2014, I formally ordained at Houston Zen Center and I received from my teacher the robes I had sewn, *dana* (generosity) bowls, and the dharma name *Gyōzan*.

During the ordination ceremony, the novice priest also receives a set of bowls called *oryoki*, which translates to "just enough." These nested bowls, wrapped in cloth, are used to receive food served during retreats, sesshins, and monastic practice. The practice of oryoki, among many things, is to remind oneself of the empty and interdependent nature of the food, the server, and the served. During the ceremony, the student's teacher will gift the person a dharma name. This name is usually of two parts, the first indicating their excellent quality or nature and the second being more aspirational, something to further actualize. My dharma name, Gyōzan Ki Shin, means "jewel mountain deep confidence." Given my past, especially my past wounds, I could not have received a more appropriate dharma name to aspire to. To see myself as precious as a gem, solid as a mountain, and deeply confident would be a far cry from where I started on the Buddhist path, but every day of the nine years that took me from anxiety to the priesthood was worth it. Every day, a dharma gate; every instance, a dharma gate. Even exiting the dharma gate is a dharma gate that keeps revolving when the time to return arrives.

LETTING THE BLOOD SPILL OUT

In the fall of 2015, I developed a loving relationship with someone living in the monastery. We decided to leave the monastery to explore whether we could be in the world together. We did that for three years, then I decided to return to the Houston Zen Center, where I remain to this day. These days, I'm engaged in many roles at the Houston Zen Center and chief among these duties is the position of assistant priest to the abbot. The center is a beautiful, thriving, and energetic temple. We hold multiple retreats throughout the year, offer a multitude of classes taught by skillful, dedicated members, and host visiting teachers and guests from far and wide.

On most Mondays, a small group of us (sometimes together, sometimes solo) make the 160-mile round trip to a maximum-security prison, Jim Ferguson Unit. Here, the "New Jim Crow" of mass incarceration of African-descended men can be witnessed firsthand. The sangha there is, in fact, a multiracial group of men. Their earnest, sincere practice mirrors what we are doing in the "free world"—the transformation of suffering and the cultivation of wisdom and compassion. I consider it a privilege to practice with these men, and I receive nourishment from their courage and openheartedness. I am forever reminded that, with just one bad decision or two, I might have joined their ranks— wearing prison whites instead of my robe. I am also reminded that imprisonment is not just due to guilt but mistaken identity, poor legal representation, a lack of financial resources, the prison industrial complex, a lack of governmental funding for treating mental illness, dysfunctional family dynamics, and slavocracy.

My Way Seeking Mind story, the story of how I came to Zen, is now fifteen years long, but it's timeless from karmic and intergenerational perspectives. My story crosses continents, nations, races, histories, economic reversals, identities, and careers. Cutting meat and cutting my wrist helped me also cut through my psychological defenses against examining past pains. But being a butcher also helped me jettison the self-loathing that prevented me from the insight that I could be a solid and confident black man in this world, even with police brutality and the prison industrial complex. This path was paved with lots of bloodletting, but the blood was mixed with the metaphorical spring waters of Zen. From the cutting board to the cushion and back again eventually led to me letting go of the cutting board. As a Zen priest in residence, I, along with the entire community, create and maintain space for anyone who needs to let their metaphorical blood spill out.

In the meantime, if reading about Zen, Buddhism, racialized trauma, or African American history is what you need to do, just as I did nine years ago, my recommended reading list for you includes the following books.

> *A Comprehensive Manual of Abhidhamma* by Bhikkhu
> Bodhi
> *The Lotus Sutra: A Contemporary Translation of a
> Buddhist Classic* translated by Gene Reeves
> *Insight Meditation: The Practice of Freedom* by Joseph
> Goldstein
> *My Grandmother's Hands: Racialized Trauma and the
> Pathway to Mending Our Hearts and Bodies* by
> Resmaa Menakem
> *Radical Dharma: Talking Race, Love, and Liberation* by
> Rev. angel Kyodo williams, Lama Rod Owens with
> Jasmine Syedullah
> *Satipatthana: The Direct Path to Realization* by Anālayo

Shobogenzo: Treasury of the True Dharma Eye by Eihei
   Dōgen
*The Warmth of Other Suns: The Epic Story of America's
   Great Migration* by Isabel Wilkerson
*Wisdom of Buddha: The Samdhinirmocana Mahayana
   Sutra* translated by John Powers
Zen Training: Methods and Philosophy by Katsuki Sekida

· 7 ·

ON BEING LAILAH'S DAUGHTER

Blessons from Umieversity on Actualizing Enlightenment

KAMILAH MAJIED

The great ocean is shallow compared to the
profoundness of the debt you owe your mother.[1]
—NICHIREN DAISHONIN, "The Four Virtues and
the Four Debts of Gratitude"

My Umi said shine a light on the world.[2]
—MOS DEF, "Umi Says"

SO MUCH OF WHAT my mother said and embodied as a Buddhist and as a Black scholar was both a lesson and a blessing that I have to create new language to describe it. The words in existence don't suffice, so I invoke this new word that speaks to the blessings and lessons I inherit from her: *Blessons*. Benedictions that were also teachings and lectures that were also aspirations—these are what I carry in my heart from my mother. They are the lights that keep me on track in the day-to-day course of revealing my own enlightenment.

I remember being in college at Mount Holyoke and one of my friends overhearing me talking to my mother on the phone. After I hung up, my friend commented, "Wow, you have a real cool mom—she lets you call her 'homie.'" I burst out laughing. When I could stop laughing, I explained to my friend that I was calling my mother *Umie*, which is Arabic for "mother" or "my mother." Umie was so generous, so nurturing to our friends, acquaintances, and even strangers that when she walked down the street, people we didn't even know would say, *"As salaam alaikum*, Umie!" or "Hi, Umie!"

When I was born in 1965, my mother was a practicing Muslim. She raised my brothers, sister, and I to be deeply spiritual from birth. I prayed five times a day, fasted, and wore the hijab to embody reverence for my spirit and divinity at all times. I remember being scared one night when I was around nine or ten, in that random way children are frightened for no tangible reason, and my mother telling me to read the Qur'an. I look back on this and remember that she did not sit there and read it with me. Rather, she directed me to seek out wisdom and solace myself, thus training me to grow my seeking mind, my mind of faith, throughout my life.

During my early childhood, Umie was a teacher and administrator of our local faith-based Islamic elementary school. As vice principal, she made sure the curriculum contained books about real history, not the "twistory" articulated by white supremacy wherein white people "discovered" the world and "developed" it. I learned about Nat Turner before I learned about Christopher Columbus, and from reading authenticated historical accounts, I understood that Nat Turner was a freedom fighter and Christopher Columbus was a genocidal rapist. The clarity I have about the contributions of Black, Asian, Latino, and Native peoples, our centrality and stewardship of the entire world despite colonization and enslavement, was impressed upon me and my siblings at an early age because of my mother.

I remember reading *I Know Why the Caged Bird Sings* when I was six and being *over the moon* in love with Maya Angelou—

and also curious about this Paul Laurence Dunbar guy whose poem that book title is from. I could not wait for Umie to take us back to East Orange Public Library (our family weekend and after-school hangout) so I could get all their books! Alice Walker, Toni Morrison, and my dearest of all, James Baldwin, lay in wait for me at the library. Having found them, for me, they became lifelong guideposts to my most liberated self, my fundamental enlightenment.

Umie encouraged my siblings and me to read constantly, and she herself was the most voracious reader I have ever known. My grandaunt Essie told me that as a child, my mother won a prize for reading all the fiction books at Red Hook Public Library in Brooklyn, where she had grown up.

When I was eight years old, I asked Umie why we had to go to bed early when we did something wrong. By way of an answer, she smiled and handed me Dostoyevsky's *Crime and Punishment*. It's hilarious now, when I look back on it. I remember squinting at her, befuddled at the time, but then feeling quite sympathetic for poor Rodion while I read the book. It was around that same time that she gave me *Anna Karenina*. I was so pleased that she trusted me with all the scandal between Anna and the Count. "Hot stuff!" I thought. Yet at the same time, I realized Umie believed not only that I could comprehend the complexity of adult relationships but also that it was never too soon for me to start understanding that complexity. She was always available to answer my questions about the books I read. She told me that, in addition to reading the canons of African diaspora literature, Asian literature, and the literature of Latin America, I had to read all the Russian classics to consider myself truly literate. She taught me that literacy was not static, that it involved ongoing dynamic engagement with the world of books.

It was Umie's hand that guided me to and through the transition from practicing Islam to practicing Buddhism. In many ways, it was not a big leap. Chanting NAM MYOHO RENGE KYO, the invocation of enlightenment that is both title and essence of the Lotus Sutra, seemed a natural developmental step in our spiritual evolution. Having recited the Al-Fatihah, since I could speak, vocalizing as spiritual practice in a language that was not English did not seem foreign. I also understood from my mother's multilingual literacy (and multilingual reprimands!) that some points, some truths, needed to be said in their original language to resonate in my life as they were meant to.

One of the greatest blessons I encountered from watching Umie was her embodiment of the importance of not just gaining knowledge but also transforming it into wisdom. Never arrogant about how well-read she was, Umie embodied an understanding that knowledge was essentially neutral and that only when knowledge is used for good, with compassion to alleviate suffering for oneself and others, could one turn the stone of knowledge into the gem of wisdom. Although she stressed the importance of learning every day of our lives, knowledge was only ever the soil from which wisdom was meant to grow. Umie tended to the development of our interior lives as assiduously as she nurtured our physical bodies. She employed literature, arts, and prayer in her architecture of our faith in our own inherent dignity and in the dignity of all life.

My mother's love of and insistence upon reading paralleled and was reinforced by the perspective of the Buddhist leader and Soka Gakkai's international president, Daisaku Ikeda, who says:

> Reading is a dialog with oneself; it is self-reflection, which cultivates profound humanity. Reading is therefore essential to our development. It expands and enriches the personality like a seed that germinates after a long time and sends forth many blossom-laden branches. People who can say of a book, "this changed my life" truly understand the meaning of happiness. Reading that sparks inner revolution is desperately needed to escape drowning in the rapidly advancing information society. Reading is more than intellectual ornamentation; it is a battle for the establishment for the self, a ceaseless challenge that keeps us young and vigorous.[3]

But it was not just through sharing literature that my mother blessed me into knowing the world and my connection to it. It was also through music.

"GOOD MORNING HEARTACHE"

I would watch Umie listening to "Good Morning Heartache" by Billie Holiday, with a whimsical look on her face, shaking her head as she sang the lyrics.[4] Little did I know, as a child, that this was a meditation practice wherein my mother used the music to guide her in reconciling with the fact that sadness often wakes up with us and in us in the morning. She was teaching me that grief was natural and that worrying often makes us sweat every outfit choice, hairstyle, comment, job application, conversation, etc., from the moment we wake up. I was young, but I got the message. Since sorrow and anxiety are part of our human experience, part of what flows through our minds constantly, we might as well make friends with sorrow and anxiety and learn to soothe them rather than trying to throw them out of the house of our minds.

I knew the sadness was there for a reason, particularly for me as a Black girl and for Black women overall, who live with the grief of being judged and treated as less valuable on a daily basis. I also knew about the grief of losing many loved ones due to health disparities arising from racism. I knew so many types of grief. I knew the pain of all that weighs on the heart even when things are going well. It's like a constant hum, an undercurrent that makes us wonder how long any moment of joy is going to last. When we meet a new friend, sadness about previous relationships gone wrong is often right there, as is fear that this one, too, will fail.

To me, "Good Morning Heartache" and many other songs my mother sang, said, "What if we were to turn toward the sadness and welcome it?" To appreciate the part of ourselves that is still hopeful enough to *get* sad and worry. Some of us are hurt beyond sadness or worry. Some of us are stuck in rage, despair, or some pretense that everything is cool. When we can feel sadness or worry, it means we are whole and connected to our hearts. So,

I started thinking perhaps when grief arises, we could offer ourselves these meditations:

Thank you, sorrow, for showing me how big my heart is and how valuable what I am grieving has been to me.

Grief is a window that allows me to look back at all that I have had, all that I have been, and all that I have loved and treasured. I am grateful to be able to grieve such wonderful experiences.

Often when I allow the tears to come, what lies beyond them is an understanding of what I still have from what was lost. The lost lover may have broken the trust, but they also showed me I could survive and maybe even learn to trust again. The lost friendship still left me with laughter and memories that will forever enrich my life. The lost job left me with experience and wisdom I can use going forward.

Because of racism and sexism, Black women have more to grieve and be anxious about than most women, and the data from disciplines ranging from economics to education and medicine bear this out. We worry about whether we are attractive enough because of sexism, which says our physical beauty *is* our value. We worry about whether we are smart enough because few people have affirmed our intellect, and it is always being questioned. We worry about getting verbally assaulted (aka, catcalled) by men who think we find that enjoyable. We worry about the pay gap, the weight gain, the relationship status, environmental racism, and we worry about our loved ones whom we are always trying to lift as we climb. Although it is necessary and valuable to fight against the injustices that give us so much worry and grief, we can also learn to live peacefully with these feelings as they arise in our hearts and minds.

Someone once said, "Anxiety is excitement without the breath." What this means to me is that if I can breathe through the anxiety, I can recognize that it is a friend trying to warn me when it thinks I am in danger. Unfortunately, it is sometimes the *very traumatized* friend—lingering anxiety in me, launched by something awful someone said or did—that is emerging at times when there is no immediate threat. I learned if I could see free-floating anxiety as my traumatized friend who is always with me, I can learn to breathe through the terror I experience so viscerally and transform trepidation into curiosity. We can offer our traumatized friends within both consolation and encouragement using this affirmation:

Thank you, anxiety, for helping me stay alert to the multiple emotional, physical, and spiritual threats in the world. You can relax, as I am breathing through the worry.

It can also be useful to breathe deeply and simply *notice* the anxiety, as opposed to claiming it as our identity. We can say to ourselves, "Oh, hello, anxiety, I feel you floating through me," instead of saying, "I am anxious."

We can recognize that worry does not prepare us for pain but rather exhausts us such that when pain comes, we are often too tired to deal with it. Realizing this, we can release worry with every out breath.

Breathing in, I notice there is anxiety; breathing out, I let it go. Breathing in, I notice risk; breathing out, I welcome opportunity.

In one of her YouTube videos, the writer and spoken word artist Jae Nichelle speaks about how her anxiety pushes her to make odd decisions. In a beautiful poem, she asks, "What happens to a Black girl who is too anxious to ever feel like magic? / Can she still fly? / Can she still be fly / with wings that tremble?"[5] She talks about her body shaking because she is always pushing against her anxiety, sweating because she is fighting an invisible boxing match against anxiety to simply *be* in the world.

What if, when we recognize that this is our experience, we welcome it? What if we used meditations such as the following?

*I welcome my trembling heart and body, as I am a tree with
firm roots. If I fall, the earth of all those who love me will
catch me.*

*With sweat and tears, I can always wash myself clean of fear
and sorrow.*

Billie Holiday—Black, female, and an utter genius, facing racism and sexism in the 1940s—offers timeless lessons to humanity in her music about negotiating pain. By learning from Ms. Holiday's wisdom, while swaying to the sound of her voice as she sings, we can invite our traumatized minds to get comfortable and have a meditation with us. From Umie, I learned that we can welcome pain, ease it within ourselves when it is standing up shouting for our attention. We can simply say, as Billie Holiday does in the last line of that song, "Good morning heartache, sit down."

I think my mother loved Billie Holiday so much because her life and music epitomized Umie's credo. Umie often said, "Life is in the nature of a struggle. You have to learn to enjoy the struggle and transform suffering into growth, progress, or something of value." Trying to wrap words around the ineffable treasures bequeathed to me by my mother—most auspiciously, the "jewel in the robe" that is Buddhism—is so unwieldly a task, so labyrinthine a process, that I don't know where to start or how to frame our story. What occurs to me is that the story is already scaffolded by the four sufferings of birth, aging, sickness, and death. Umie used her enlightened wisdom to catalyze my own as we moved through the four sufferings together.

BIRTH, AGING, SICKNESS, AND DEATH

I know I cannot tell the story of birth, aging, sickness, and death in four separate sections, or as "four meetings," the way Shakyamuni Buddha described it. Because of the health disparities faced by my Black family, to meet one of these sufferings often meant to meet the others at the same time or soon thereafter.

When I was born, segregation was newly outlawed yet still commonly practiced. When my mother once described to me how callous and dismissive the doctors were during her seventy-two-hour labor in a segregated ward of a New York City hospital, I thought about a scene in Toni Morrison's *The Bluest Eye*. In that scene, Pecola's mother, Pauline, is in labor when the white doctor treats her roughly, saying to his interns, "These here women you don't have any trouble with. They deliver right away and with no pain. Just like horses."[6] I think about how terrified my mother had to be giving birth, having already lost her older sister in childbirth two years prior under medically negligent circumstances.

I recently heard a television report from a Harvard study detailing how Black women in the United States have much higher rates of maternal mortality than white women.[7] When I heard this, my chest started pounding and I did not know how to feel—I just had to leave the room. But I couldn't get out of the room before hearing that not only does the United States have the highest rate of maternal mortality in the "developed" world but that Black women are also *three to four times* more likely than white women to die in childbirth. When asked why, Dr. Neel Shah, one of the lead researchers, said it was *not* due to having less education or money, as those variables were controlled for in the studies. He said it was because "we believe black women less when they are expressing concerns about the symptoms they're having, particularly around pain."[8]

At my altar, I chanted and tried to hold this information in my heart while thinking about my mother's *other* sister, who *also* died in childbirth. My second aunt died over a decade later, in 1981. I was fifteen then, and I remember thinking about how giving birth is supposed to be a time when a woman is honored and supported in her labor and how, instead, both my aunts suffered indescribably and died without ever holding their newborns. For them, the birth of their child was a time when their suffering was ignored. Because of that ignorance, it was the time when their lives were ending—even as they brought new life into the world.

Their deaths shaped my family, as my mother took her deceased sisters' children and raised them as my siblings. Umie's compassion and courage shined through the pain of losing her beloved sisters. She decided, despite being a single mother of five already, that she had room in her heart and her life to raise her sisters' children as her own. I remember her telling us that this loss was terrible and that our household was growing because of it—that we were to fill in and fill up the space left by my second aunt's death. My mother made it clear we were to make room in our hearts and our home for one another, and as a family, we were going to grow from this suffering too.

A year after her second sister's death, Umie began practicing Buddhism. It was clear that she was going deeper spiritually to access more interior wealth that would allow her to manage her new responsibilities. It was also around this same time that, despite working full-time and raising the six of us, she decided to go to law school. I saw so much ebullient joy in her as she navigated all this that it made me decide to start practicing Buddhism, too, that same year.

Three years later when I was a rising junior returning to college after a summer at home, I remember noticing my mother's pride tinged with mild astonishment and indignation. After we'd finished unloading my things from the car outside my dormitory, she looked at me and exclaimed, "Youth is so arrogant!" I cannot remember what I did or said to make her say that, but I am sure that I was full of youthful insouciance (or full of something) as I casually bid her adieu at a moment that was, for her, a very significant departure. Looking back, I know now I resisted any whiff of sentimentality from my mother because I so loathed to see her cry. I'd seen her cry so much. I'd watched her cry out from the bone-aching pain caused by severe sickle cell anemia crises, which had required her to be hospitalized every single year of my life. I'd watched her cry over heartbreaking financial setbacks as she worked to dream our futures into existence. I'd watched her cry at the loss of so many loved ones. I'd watched her weep through the loss of her own mother before I was ten years old. I'd watched her grieve my brother, who died when he was just twelve years old of complications related to sickle cell anemia.

I'd also watched her use her spiritual practice to buoy her life and ours in the face of all these storms of loss. And I'd watched her enact the teaching offered by Daisaku Ikeda: "Health is not simply the absence of illness. Real health is the will to overcome every form of adversity and use even the worst of circumstances as a springboard for new growth and development. Simply put, the essence of health is the constant renewal and rejuvenation of life."[9]

The untimely deaths of my two aunts, my brother, and my grandmother were not the only shocking losses our family faced. Two of my uncles died young, as did my magnificent grandfather, leaving only my mother and her youngest brother from any previous generation in my family. Health disparities reflecting the inequalities in health care for Black people swept through my family like a war, far worse than a plague, such that when my mother died at sixty, when I was forty years old, I became the de facto matriarch of my family.

The disparate medical treatment that has savaged my family is still evident when I go to the doctor now. I see how prone the doctors are to sum me up without even listening to me, and how I have to push back to be seen—really seen and heard—by doctors. A 2016 study showed that 25 percent of medical residents thought Black people actually have thicker skin, and 14 percent thought we have thicker nerve endings—both of which they believed make us less sensitive to pain. I consider how these false beliefs impacted the aging, illness, and deaths of my beloved aunts, grandparents, uncles, and other family members. Racism exacerbates the four sufferings for Black people and makes sickness or aging an almost certain predictor of untimely death—far more so than they do for white people.

I juxtapose this with the ways I actually have learned to live with pain and tolerate more pain than I should. And I wonder if this is a reflection of internalized racism—me having to be tougher because I am perceived as such. If so, that is part of the story of my resilience, the story of strength I have built through practicing Buddhism. Yet, I still use my Buddhist practice to know when *not* to push through pain.

BEYOND THE FOUR SUFFERINGS: SOARING INTO ETERNITY

It is because of my practice that I can feel the enlightened wisdom and presence of my mother with me in everything I do. I look back on that day outside my dorm and understand that she was not complaining. She was marveling at how little we understand about impermanence when we are young—and she was correct.

When the doctors told me that my mother was dying—that it was moments away, not hours any more—it was just her and me in the room. I took her hand and said, "Let's recite the Lotus Sutra together one more time." She passed during that recitation, and I remember how extraordinarily dignified she looked, how nobly serene. I kissed her hand and said, "Bless these hands that braided my hair and taught me to write." I kissed her feet and said, "Bless these feet that walked me to school and to prayer." I kissed her belly and said, "Bless this body that I came through." I kissed her chest and said, "Bless this heart that loved so many so well." I kissed her forehead and said, "Bless this mind from which my own grew."

Wild grief scorched through me as I exited the hospital to face a stunning dawn, one so picturesque that it seemed gaudy in the face of the incommunicable gloom I felt. Yet because of Umie, because of both her life and her death, I understood the four sufferings and impermanence from a perspective more visceral and profound than I ever had before. Umie showed me that being brilliant is not about how bright you are but how bright a light you shine on everyone and everything around you. Her life as a formal and informal educator taught me to shine a light on the world and everyone I come in contact with, and thereby to illuminate the shining, cosmic brilliance innate in everyone and everything. She taught me to live life bravely and with an open heart. She wrote these words in the volume of *The Major Writ-*

ings of Nichiren Daishonin that I gave her: "Lack of courage is the greatest impediment to happiness."

It is her courage that allows me to write through tears to tell some portion of our story. When Daisaku Ikeda talks about his mentor Jōsei Toda, he says that their lives have coalesced; they breathe together. I breathe in this moment with and for my mother. I know that her life force is with me still. I believe she is always functioning as a protective factor in the universe and that she has not come embodied in another human form yet. Maybe it is just wishful thinking, but I am hoping that she is waiting for the right time so that she can be my mother again in our next shared physical existence. And now, when I see a psychedelic sky all decked out in fuchsia and purple hues, I know that my mother's life force is elemental, that she is painting the sky for me. She is reminding me that I am the writer, set designer, and star player in the ongoing story of our life, and that she has my back, always.

My mentor in Buddhism, Daisaku Ikeda, writes, "Even in death the life state of Buddhahood possesses the cosmic life and the power to exercise infinite compassion. Buddhahood is infinite and eternal whether in life or death." I know this to be true as I encounter people and have experiences that allow me to share the blessons I continue to receive from the Umieverse. Her life force endures. Her brilliant, enlightened mind infuses my mind, and her heart ever-expands my heart, blessing me into wisdom eternally.

· 8 ·

WHOLENESS IS NO TRIFLING MATTER

Race, Faith, and Refuge

RUTH KING

Are you sure, sweetheart, that you want to be well?
... cause wholeness is no trifling matter.[1]
—TONI CADE BAMBARA, *The Salt Eaters*

WHILE PARTICIPATING in a six-week dream workshop in Santa Cruz, California, in 1985, long before I discovered the dharma, I had a powerful dream. I saw myself sitting on a flower in the middle of a still lake—full, round, and content. The sun was shining, the birds were singing my favorite song, *and* there was a torrential storm. The thunder roared shaming voices from the past, and the lightning, with etchings of chiseled faces and body parts, unforgivingly struck the full of my body. Yet my experience was one of calm, clarity, and contentment. I was not shaken or disturbed in the least. The dream seemed without end, and I awoke with a steadiness I had never known.

Before this taste of ease, I had lived in a sea of suffering.

FIRST NOBLE TRUTH: THERE IS SUFFERING

Family

I grew up in the 1950s and 1960s, in the heat of the Civil Rights movement in south central Los Angeles, in an atmosphere of fear, violence, and jazz. In our working-class community in which many families like ours managed to own their own homes, we grew up knowing we were hated by white people, and our ambition was survival.

The way my single-parent mom managed eight kids, and her own vulnerability, was through high control and severe punishment. And I was the "sensitive" one, the crybaby. This meant I got my ass kicked often because it was dangerous to show vulnerability in my family and community. To be sensitive was to be a target of harm.

I covered up my tenderness with toughness, but I was never good at it. Of the many fights I found myself in, I don't recall ever winning one. Little did I know back then that winning a fight would become my ambition.

Our family was active in the Civil Rights movement, the NAACP, and Urban League, which were fighting against job discrimination, police brutality, and advocating for equal voting rights. My mother's light skin gave her privileges that many dark-skinned people didn't have, and it was a common political strategy for light-skinned people to gain access to jobs and then insist on fair treatment for other Black people. But this resulted in job instability as she would often get fired for organizing and "making trouble." This volatility heightened tension and fear in our home and community.

Growing up, racism impinged on every aspect of well-being in our lives and the lives around us. But as a child, what was more palpable was the strict control and lack of safety I felt in my family, and the fear, hurt, and rage I had to swallow to survive it. I recall thinking often, *I can't wait to get out of here!*

My great-grandmother worried constantly about not being able to protect all of us from the horrors of racism and poverty. She would pace back and forth in her kitchen mumbling and praying in a soiled apron. I remember being so small and feeling intensely disturbed about her worry, mainly because I couldn't comfort her. I was seven when she died of what I believe was a broken heart, and there was a part of me that whispered, *There's got to be a better way.*

My mother, on the other hand, appeared to be a pro at facing loss and disappointment. By the time she was twenty-four, she had lost her mother, three of her siblings (whom she had been responsible for raising), and her father, *and* she had six children of her own to raise. And she managed it all with a steely grit. In fact, her capacity to handle everything frightened me. When army officers drove up to our house to inform us of my uncle's death, before they reached the door, my mother retreated to her room, fell on her knees, and moaned in prayer. She then answered the door composed, dignified, and clear.

I couldn't understand how anyone could do what she did time and time again and survive it. My mom had unshakable faith in God. As a child, I could not imagine having that much faith in anything or anyone.

Like so many of us, I felt the heat of my light before I knew its power. As a child, this energy felt like a voracious animal pacing around inside me, always on the prowl. It was as if, 24/7, my insides were burning, and I knew instinctively that this energy was dangerous and needed to be kept under wraps.

Church

We were raised in the church. My mom was the choir director and pianist, and all the girls sang in the choir. My oldest sister could sing the gospel so forcefully, I was convinced she was having an argument with my mom, who played staccato-like chords in response. I loved the spirit of the songs more than the words. The spirit of the songs felt more like acupressure points that freed the flow of energy and aligned with a vibrational truth that sent chills up your spine and made everyone's faces shine like the high-noon sun.

The church was always a place of wonder to me; it represented fear and care at the same time. The emphasis on obedience and damnation was palpable. At the same time, people could get happy with the holy ghost, dance and shout—fall out, even—and be so tenderly cared for, unjudged, and well fed. And while the church spoke of faith, the church didn't teach me how to navigate the weight of my life and the lives around me. It all felt confusing, imprisoning and impossible, edgy and desperate, and, like Forrest Gump, I just wanted to run!

Teenage Mom

At age fifteen, I became pregnant. It was not uncommon for members of my family or my community to be teenage mothers. I was determined to stay in school and participated in a program that allowed me to continue high school and graduate with my class, with my son on my hip. I was in love for a hot minute with the father of my son, whom I married, but it was never really about him. I later came to understand that I married primarily as a way out of my family home.

While I had no clue how I was going to pull off motherhood, during my pregnancy I felt beautiful, sensually alive, vibrant, powerful, vulnerable, and fearless. Naivete has this kind of power. After giving birth, I remember asking my mom, "Why is it that I feel excited about this baby, yet so frightened?" And she replied, "Because you've brought another black boy into this world. Buckle up!"

This didn't help, but it didn't take long to understand what she meant. I was raised to distrust white people. My mother would explain to us often that white people were not taught to care for black bodies, only exploit them, and with little consequence. Though I was still so young and had so much life ahead of me, I had now joined the ranks of struggling black mothers who could not control their destiny—nor the destinies of their sons.

Father's Murder

When I was seventeen, on the very day the Watts riots broke out, my father was murdered by his girlfriend in a jealous rage. She went virtually unpunished.

His death emotionally paralyzed me. I wouldn't say I had a strong relationship with my father. He and my mother had been long divorced by this time and he had become a prominent businessman, a successful plumber with a growing business. I didn't long for a relationship with him. It was normal that he was not in my life. But I expected to feel *something* when he died. For years, I thought it odd that I was pretty much numb to his murder. What I didn't realize is that numb and cold are actually feelings.

At his funeral, as I held tight to my then two-year-old son as the procession was stopped several times by the National Guard because of all the rioting, all I could think was that a black life didn't seem to matter much. Not that this was a big revelation. And even though I saw the evidence of this truth everywhere around me from white folks, I could not, at the time, reconcile how a black woman could kill my father and get away with it. I was more disturbed by this than I could admit to myself.

Three Strikes: Illness

Not only did my mother not trust white folks, like so many Black people of her generation, but she also didn't trust the health care system farther than you could spit. She had had too many friends and family members go into the hospital for a simple procedure and never return home. Following her lead, I tended to avoid doctors, and for this reason, my hyperactive thyroid went undiagnosed for many years. I treated my ravenous hunger as normal and played it out in hypersexuality and ambition, without realizing I was *also* ill. It was the early sixties, after all: the age of the sexual revolution.

When I was finally diagnosed and treated for hyperthyroidism at age twenty-two (the large lump in my throat an undeniable sign), the doctor explained that the hyperactivity had enlarged my heart; I would likely need open-heart surgery. Convinced that my mother was right, I ignored him and went on about the business of surviving.

Two years later, I had a hysterectomy: my fibroid tumors had given me tremendous pain for a number of years, and this time, I followed the doctor's advice. But upon awakening from the surgery to find myself in a ward full of Black women in their early twenties, all of whom had recently had hysterectomies, I felt disturbed and alarmed once again. It was clear a conspiracy against black bodies was, indeed, at play. My mother was right again.

And then came the life-threatening heart surgery for a mitral valve prolapse. I'm told it was congenital, although I think it was from all the rage and fear I had been trying to deny. The irony isn't lost on me that I entrusted white surgeons with my heart. I'd say that at that point in my life they had more access to it than I did.

My mother was deeply disturbed by my decision to have heart surgery. The night before my surgery, she filled my hospital room with every healer and holy person she knew. I was surrounded by the most beautiful healing circle. Surprisingly, my oldest sister, the one who had so terrified me as a child, sat vigil all night, braiding my hair and humming soothing songs.

The next thing I knew, I was awake from surgery and told that they did not have to replace the valve after all; they were able to repair it. Of course, my mother attributed it to prayer, not surgical skill. And perhaps she was right!

The surgical procedure left me needing to relearn how to breathe. I didn't have energy to think, only heal, and I had to lie very still. The weight of the life I had been living was now sitting right on top of me. I wasn't in control, and I realized I never had been. And then, with rest, I began to live more in my body, perhaps for the first time.

Ambition

I had gone to work right out of high school, desperate to be free from my family and recent divorce. I was determined to never look back or go back. Within three years of graduation, I had moved my son from the jungles of south central Los Angeles to Altadena and purchased my first home at the age of twenty-one through a HUD program. It took me close to eighteen months to come up with the $1,500 down payment, $500 of which my brother loaned me.

I went through relationships like cough drops. I had a PhD in endings. I was angry, eruptive, agitated, as if allergic to skin, and I was at war with anyone and everyone who dared to get close to me.

One of my jobs was as a secretary in a community mental health agency, where I discovered that people like me could be supported through therapy. Because I had a relationship with the people I worked with, I began to talk about my fears and struggles. It was odd to be met with care and patience instead of judgment, and the impact was immediate; I experienced a release of tension I hadn't even realized I was holding. It was as if the grip of rage had loosened. I felt lighter and more spacious. More profoundly, I realized this was something I could give myself. I began to see how what happened so-called "back then" wasn't left behind but rather was still alive here and now. Through understanding the roots of my worry, I could be less controlled by habitual and reactive responses.

This was the age of affirmative action, and my natural talent for teaching led to an offer to become a human resources training assistant within TRW, a credit reporting business. I'm sure a yellow-skinned black woman felt less threatening than a darker-skinned sister to the white folks who hired me.

This corporation would, within two years, sponsor me in Pepperdine University's master's program in organizational development, but I became so enraged with the racist establishment at Pepperdine that I completed the coursework short of the dissertation and left the program. Granted, there was racism within the system, but I was also physically and mentally unstable. By leaving, I took care of one of the issues: removing myself from the racist institution. However, racism wreaked havoc on my heart.

Aka, Lesbian

The Pepperdine graduate program met every six weeks in an off-campus location in the Santa Cruz mountains of California. The beauty of that place stunned me; I had never seen so many colors of green in trees. Compelled by the beauty and in the thick of much upheaval in my life, I up and moved to Santa Cruz. It helped that I had also fallen in love with a woman in my graduate program who lived in Santa Cruz. This was unexpected—but not really!

I think I was nine when I had my first inkling that I might be attracted to women. I was in the car with my mom, stopped at a red light. I glanced over at the woman in the car to our right. She was stunningly attractive. Our eyes met just as the light was turning green, and she winked at me as she drove off. I was riveted with pleasure. I glanced over at my mom, no doubt beaming brightly, and she had this look on her face that said, *Don't you ever let me catch you looking at women that way again.*

Twenty-five years later, here I was, reunited with that flicker of joy, now a blazing light of freedom, exhilaration, and unquestionable clarity.

Spiritual Explorations

About a year after my move, I entered a master's program in clinical psychology at John F. Kennedy University and continued exploring my new life as a lesbian in Santa Cruz. I found myself interested in metaphysical, psychological, cosmological, shamanic, and feminist spiritual practices. My sense of what religion could be was being broadened beyond the Baptist church. It was during this time that I had the dream that opened this piece.

I had many questions and sought understanding from many spiritual traditions. A shaman from the Appalachian Mountains of Ohio conducted a past life reading and told me that before coming into this life, I had been silent for forty-five years, and that I was so resistant to coming out of silence into this life that my heart stopped beating in the birth passage, then began again.

This information shed new light on the origin of my open-heart surgery experience, which was originally framed as congenital. I questioned, *Could the surgery have actually been a repair from a previous life wounding?*

Suffering: Connecting Dots

In the early eighties, I was recruited by Intel Corporation to head up their organizational development division, supporting leaders to understand power and diversity dynamics in the thick of multiple mergers and acquisitions. I was good at what I did, but it came wrapped in righteous rage. The simplest of matters felt like life-or-death. The corporation, unconscious of the racism it breeds, did feel like a war zone, and I was beginning to question how much of it was my own creation. It wasn't like I felt better when I won a fight. It was that I was always looking for one.

For years, I used my position to challenge white dominance within corporations, constantly pushing on systemic practices that kept me and others like me unheard and undervalued. It was exhausting work and I often felt ill. And I was also painfully aware that my struggles were a modern-day version of what my parents and their parents had experienced throughout their lives, and that what I had inherited was not only the persistent issue of racism but also the "struggle" I experienced and created in relationship to it.

The intricate splinters of racism were a living and daily horror, and my response was still wrapped in aggression and hatred toward others and myself. I felt like I was over-functioning and wasting away. My efforts were not working, and I couldn't stop trying. I hid how unsafe I felt, how desperate I felt, and how intolerable the situation often was. I felt disconnected and imprisoned by my thoughts, and I couldn't see a way out of my disease. No amount of faith, as I had come to know it, supported a sustained shift from this inner distress and distrust. This hellhole norm, in fact, felt like violence. And I began to ask, *Why are you doing this? Is it for peace?*

Travel Medicine

In my profession I was able to travel internationally, and then when work was over, I traveled for fun, mostly to experience different cultures and spiritual traditions. I led cultural exchange tours for a few years to South Africa, Ghana, Senegal, and Kemet (Egypt). During one journey to Johannesburg, shortly after Nelson Mandela was elected president, I met with over a dozen NGO leaders who had fought against apartheid and for Nelson Mandela. It was amazing to sit with them, feel their fire, and understand their devotion, faith, and resilience in this generational struggle. I asked each of them a naive question: "What will you do now that apartheid has legally ended?" The response from most was, "I don't know. I've never thought about that." I felt deeply troubled by their responses.

What is the end game? Is it fighting against racism or fighting for peace? Is there ever an end? I was clear that I didn't want to be absorbed in what was wrong without knowing where I wanted to go. I was clear that I didn't want to be afraid or to live in constant turmoil. Even more frightening, I was clear I was tired of fighting. Fighting seemed endless and someone was bound to get hurt. I couldn't help but think about the traumatic wounds that had been passed down from many generations of struggle, the wounds I had experienced, and the handicap I lived with fighting with invisible, forgotten, and unhealed scars—the kind of wounding that robs you of dreams beyond suffering.

Life wasn't all doom and gloom, however. Moving to Northern California, feeling new sexual and spiritual freedom, healing and becoming more regulated from the imbalances of hyperthyroidism and open-heart surgery, and enjoying the breadth of world travel were transformative and inspiring. Change, and its inevitability, felt like freedom.

During this same period, I took a six-week trip to South India with a small group of women to study the stories of the textiles, view ancient architecture, and watch classical dances. When our connecting flight was delayed, we were put up in what seemed like an abandoned hotel near Cochin International Airport. Our group was to meet in the lobby at 4:30 a.m. A friend in our group and I were the only ones who showed up on time in the lobby. How fortunate, too, because suddenly a sea of saffron and gold swirled by, and in the center of this swirl was His Holiness the Dalai Lama. He locked eyes with me for a second or two, but it felt like a lifetime. This glance so pure, quiet, swift, and piercing, felt like a lightning bolt of love and acceptance.

I trembled and cried for days; there were no words. I recall thinking, *Here's proof! In this flawed world, it is possible to look upon others with pure heartedness and acceptance.* I knew nothing of this man, but I wanted to feel what he evoked in me forever!

During my travels, I came to appreciate the devotional practices of Hindus as well as the spiritual traditions of Santeria and Yoruba of West Africa, Cuba, Brazil, Haiti, and North America. I was fascinated to see what appeared to be a seamless and natural integration of cultural and spiritual responsibility. And while I wasn't quick to surrender to any religion or spirituality, a part of me was open to it.

SECOND NOBLE TRUTH: THERE IS A CAUSE OF SUFFERING

Turning Open

In 1992, after twenty-plus years in corporate America, I left my job to pursue a deeper understanding of freedom. I didn't know what that was exactly, but I knew what it wasn't. It wasn't staying put! It was honoring change, perhaps redefining faith, and I needed space outside of form to figure it out. Oddly, despite the uncertainty, I left the safety of paycheck and structure. Was this faith? If so, in what?

In 1995, I traveled to Beijing to attend the Women's World Conference, where I shared a training I had developed on generational healing. I had over three hundred women attendees. On a side tour, I found myself standing next to another African

American woman as we marveled at a Buddha the size of a two-story building, similar to the one I had seen in the dream ten years earlier in Santa Cruz. Both of us had long dreadlocks and tears in our eyes. This stranger turned to me and asked, "Do you meditate?" I said, "Kinda."

She introduced herself as Dr. Marlene Jones Schoonover, and within a few moments, we discovered we both lived in Northern California, not far from each other. She invited me to Spirit Rock Meditation Center to meditate with her. She was on Spirit Rock's board at the time and was struggling with diversity issues; she was looking for sisterhood. I shared that I had left my high-paying job to get *away* from organizational racism, to which she rolled her eyes and laughed.

Over months, we talked at length about our children and mothers, and whether our service was aligned with our hearts. We discussed racial ignorance in spiritual communities and our aspirations of healing the wounds that divided us. We shared how difficult it was to keep our hearts open, and she shared how much meditation practice helped. I was enchanted by this woman.

I knew by then that my habitual ways of being at war with life, and particularly how I was relating to racial distress, were not working, and her presence represented a more easeful way. I wondered if Buddhism held some answers for me.

"Yes!" to Buddhist Practice

I eventually joined Marlene one Monday night at Spirit Rock and met her teacher, Jack Kornfield, who was giving the dharma talk. He opened by saying something like this:

> Oh nobly born, you who are the sons and daughters of the Buddha—the awakened one. Remember who you are. Because the element of the truth seeker is within you, there is a part of you that already knows who you are and wants to awaken to this mystery. And because this is a part of you, it takes you on this journey of discovery.

I could feel my entire body ringing like a sweet, vibrating bell. Everything in me was screaming YES! Spiritual doubt was minuscule in the face of this moment. It was the "already knows who you are" part that rang loud. It all felt like a homecoming.

I'm not sure I heard much more of Jack's talk that evening, but in short order, Spirit Rock Meditation Center became my practice community. Marlene was the only African American woman on the board. I already knew of her deep passion for relieving the suffering of African Americans through meditation and, despite my reluctance, at Marlene's request, I joined the Spirit Rock Diversity Council, mainly to support her. Through Marlene's persistence, Spirit Rock offered the first African American meditation retreat, with close to one hundred in attendance. Shortly after the retreat, Alice Walker and Marlene formed a small sangha (a community that practices Buddhism together) of eight women of color (including me) and invited Jack Kornfield to be our teacher. I refer to this as the 8+1 Wisdom Circle.

For ten years, the 8+1 Wisdom Circle met monthly, sharing our lives and studying the Buddha's teachings. At this early stage of my practice, I was crazed and curious, asking, *How do I do what must be done in the world without causing harm to myself or to others?* This thirst, in Buddhism, is often referred to as *samvega*, an urgency toward spiritual understanding that leads to freedom.

During this time, we all attended long meditation retreats, some of them three months in length. I graduated from Spirit Rock's Dedicated Practitioner Program (a two-year immersion in the study of Buddhism) and for six years, I studied with Rinchen Gyalmo, a Tibetan Dzogchen master. I was also teaching my Celebration of Rage retreat across the nation and giving birth to my first book, *Healing Rage*, which this 8+1 Circle midwifed. Through meditation practice, I was beginning to realize that my mind—my relationship to distress—was not only a righteous and persistent oppressor but also my understanding of the nature of mind was my ticket to freedom.

It was in this 8+1 Wisdom Circle that I began to realize the Buddhist symbolism of the dream I had had in Santa Cruz all those years before: That fat and round and full figure, with my face, sitting on a flower in the middle of a still lake during a torrential storm, was my own Buddha nature. It was sitting on the lotus flower of becoming, having a peaceful war with Mara, the force of delusion and ignorance. I also was beginning to understand the medicine of compassion and how this had manifested in the Dalai Lama's "glance of mercy" toward me at that hotel in South India. Apparently, Buddhism had been flirting with me long before I realized it.

I left the 8+1 Wisdom Circle feeling spiritually nourished and well-practiced in the dharma and the fundamentals of Western Buddhist teachings. Two years later, Jack Kornfield asked me to teach the dharma, which I accepted. He put me in the loving care of Tara Brach, founder of the Insight Meditation Community of Washington, where I became a guiding teacher. By then I had moved to Charlotte, North Carolina, where I started the Mindful Members Meditation Community. I later joined the Teacher's Council of Spirit Rock Meditation Center, becoming a core teacher in Spirit Rock's two-year Dedicated Practitioner Program.

Wholeness: No Trifling Matter

As a Buddhist practitioner and teacher, I have sat on my meditation cushion in silence, with hundreds of other yogis, ripening my capacity to live in gentle and wise awareness, sometimes day after day for months at a time, without ever speaking to the yogi who sat beside me. Within me, there was comfort in knowing that despite racial appearances, we had somehow landed on our cushions and were opening our hearts together. This, in my mind, is a miracle.

But over the years, participating in dharma community mostly attended and led by white people, I have often felt my heart quake and stomach tighten after hearing white teachers and yogis speak from a lack of awareness of themselves as racial beings. I have never heard white teachers make blatant racist comments with intent to harm. Rather, there was a more subtle obliviousness about whiteness as a collective reality and its privilege and impact, and an assumption that we were all the same or wanted to be. In those moments, despite my best efforts, I would be reminded of race and of being invisible and would spin into a hurricane of anger, confusion, and despair.

Over the years, I had both experienced and witnessed intense bruising and racial distress from such ignorance, resulting in separation. This particular flavor of separation reflected not only a division of the races, but also a division of heart. The consciousness—or unconsciousness—that supports racial suffering cuts people out of our hearts. We then try to live as if "cutting" doesn't hurt. We pretend we are not bleeding from the wounds of separation as we move about our lives in search of freedom and contentment, and we have convinced ourselves that we can live disconnected—from the planet and each other—and still be whole, happy, and peaceful.

It was sobering to acknowledge that being in a sea of racial ignorance wasn't going to disappear anytime soon. Then I began to muse: Clearly, my freedom is not dependent upon whether white folks wake up to their ignorance, right? Clearly, my freedom is more immediate and in my hands, right? Right! I was reminded of what Toni Cade Bambara had written in *The Salt Eaters*:

Are you sure, sweetheart, that you want to be well? . . .
Just so's you're sure, sweetheart, and ready to be healed,
cause wholeness is no trifling matter."[2]

I asked myself, *What would it take for me to walk in a world of racial ignorance being well and being whole, and not shutting others out of my heart?* Such an idea of freedom was in my hands and became my pledge of allegiance. *No trifling matter!* And more accessible through the dharma.

But what does this mean and how does it look as we engage as a sangha—as a community?

Moving South

In 2008, the year President Obama was elected, I moved from a racially engaged and diverse community in Berkeley, California, to a racially segregated and cautious community in Charlotte, North Carolina. In Charlotte, I could feel, at my feet, the discontent of the ancestors and, at my face, a polite distance tinged with hostility.

At that time, racial tension was at an all-time high after a rash of killings of unarmed black men, women, and children by police, and there was civilian retaliation toward police officers. On one of my morning walks in Charlotte, I noticed that many of my neighbors, most of whom are white, had small American flags lining their yards in honor of the recently killed police officers. For years, I've walked this same path and never have I seen symbols of care for the masses of black lives who have so viciously lost their lives at the hasty hands of police. Strangely, on this walk in my friendly neighborhood, where I had to repeatedly replace the missing Obama/Biden sign in my front yard, I felt oddly diminished and threatened.

THIRD NOBLE TRUTH: THERE IS FREEDOM FROM SUFFERING

Dharma As Refuge: Embodying Faith

> When we can sit in the face of insanity or dislike
> and be free from the need to make it different,
> then we are free.
> —NELSON MANDELA

As I would discover, in Theravada Buddhism, mindfulness (or *vipassana* meditation) is the technology for shifting from being ensnarled in suffering to being curious about it. In this practice, we learn to know what's happening while it's happening. We get still and turn our attention inward to become more intimately aware of our body and breath, our emotions, and our thoughts.

The practice supports awareness without interference, and without distortion, elaboration, or judgment. A process, not an easy destination, to be sure. bell hooks shed a lovely light on mindfulness practice: "Knowing how to be solitary is central to the art of loving. When we can be alone, we can be with others without using them as a means of escape."³

There were many things I found powerful about mindfulness meditation—chiefly that it assumes we are noticing our experiences with an understanding that everything we are aware of has a nature, which Buddhism describes as the Three Characteristics of Existence:

- The nature of impermanence (*anicca*): change is constant and all phenomena arise and pass away.
- The nature of selflessness (*anatta*): there is no enduring or reliable self; we are a series of ever-changing elemental processes, all arising and passing away.
- The nature of unreliability, ungovernability, and dissatisfaction (*dukkha*): "Shit happens," and things won't always go our way.

Mindfulness: Life Is Not Personal, Permanent, or Perfect

I have a simple mantra for remembering these laws of nature: *life is not personal, permanent, or perfect.*

Through mindfulness meditation, I discovered that awareness can ride the energies of persistent and disturbing thoughts and emotions without interference or personalization. When I did this, I found that old traumas and pain came out of hiding, and I could then honor and dissolve them. I discovered that I could tolerate being vulnerable and rest in tenderness, and I became deeply acquainted with ease and joy, regardless of my circumstances.

Not only was this a steady and powerful realization in sitting meditation practice, but this understanding greatly impacted how I related to the harsh realities of day-to-day life. Reminding myself that life is not personal, permanent, or perfect has kept me from falling into sinkholes of despair and destroying rooms with rage. It invites me to pause and turn inward. It gives me a chance to ask myself, "What's happening? Where are you gripped right now? Are you taking this situation personally—to be a personal experience instead of a human experience? Have people before you felt this way? Where else in the world are people feeling similarly gripped? Do you believe that how it is now is how it will always be? Are you distressed because you are insisting that this situation be other than it is, right here and now? How can you care for the pain you're in at this moment?"

What freedom that was: not to be held in the tight grip of anger, defensiveness, and fear; to have a way to turn inward, to release myself from the bondage of being on red alert, always ready to have my rage engaged.

Links to Liberation: Suffering and Faith

Another core teaching within Buddhism that spun my head around and deepened my understanding of the role of suffering and faith was liberative dependent co-arising, which lays out twelve causal links to liberation. The depth of this cause-and-effect teaching is beyond the scope of this chapter; however, it was significant to me that the first of these links was suffering and the second, faith. Simply speaking, suffering creates the conditions for faith to be known. This teaching allowed me to track how this was so in my mindfulness practice, my direct experience. This was not the faith of my childhood (so full of threats of damnation) yet it contributed greatly to understanding, compassion, and forgiveness of many childhood traumas.

We need only reflect on our lives to understand the relationship that suffering has to faith. How else can we reconcile the horrors of our lives and loving acts of kindness? How else can we make sense out of savagery and purity, wickedness and compassion, dishonesty and innocence, irrationality and wisdom, distance and intimacy, or force and receptivity? It all coexists!

How sobering it was to recognize, through practice, that

every thought and action gives birth to something, and that I could influence not what arises in my mind or externally, but how I was relating to it. How relieving it was to realize such agency and its consequences, and that I can direct my heart and mind toward freedom and away from suffering.

I should say that faith does not end suffering. It makes suffering more dignified—more honest, intimate, and sacred. Perhaps faith is, as James Baldwin says, the "growing up" side of suffering.

Perception: Reinterpreting the Familiar

Buddhism teaches us to pay attention to the reinforcing mechanism of misperceiving, ways we have been mentally conditioned to distort reality. This mechanism consists of a three-part cycle: (1) We perceive through our senses: the ears hear, eyes see, nose smells, body touches, tongue tastes, and mind thinks. (2) Once we perceive, the mind habitually jumps to thoughts and feelings about what has been perceived, commonly rooted in past experiences and conditioning. Thoughts and feelings then influence the mood of our mind. (3) When perceptions, thoughts and feelings are reinforced, views and beliefs solidify; they stay intact as truth, flavoring how we experience and respond to the next moment and to the world.

Understanding this cycle of misperception has been a profound practice, impacting how I relate to racial distress in others and myself. For example, I had just taught a Mindful of Race training program in Charlottesville, Virginia, and was given a ride to the airport by a young white woman. We stopped at a signal and I looked up at the street sign and it read Barack Avenue. I suddenly felt like I was glowing, warm, and tingling. I thought, *What a progressive city!* In my mind, I had called my partner and said, "We need to move here." In my mind, I had dressed myself in regal African attire and was speaking Swahili. My view of Charlottesville had instantly shifted from the resistance to the training I had just experienced hours ago to a progressive city I could live in.

It was then that I decided to speak, and I said, "Wow, I'm impressed. You have a street named after President Barack

Obama." Her response, after a brief pause, "In these parts, we call this street Barracks Avenue." Belly laughter ensued! I had misperceived and created an entire story around it.

Imagine what would have happened if I hadn't opened my mouth. I probably would have carried that belief around and shared it with others as truth. How funny that we can be so right when we're wrong. But it's not always so funny. When we are quick to perceive—when we think we know—we stop being curious.

Perception determines the characteristics of what it perceives—for example, whether a race is threatening or whether a race is worth paying attention to. Perception determines whether we like someone or something; in an armed confrontation, it determines whether we shoot someone or pause. Through this practice of questioning my perceptions, I was able to directly discern that race is not inherently good or bad, right or wrong. It is our *judgment* about race—how we have been conditioned to think and perceive—that's problematic. This, we can do something about.

FOURTH NOBLE TRUTH:
THERE IS A PATH TO FREEDOM

Bodhisattva and the Ten Perfections

Within the Buddhist tradition, a bodhisattva is an individual who, through their actions, vows to live in service to the collective, for the welfare and awakening of all beings. In other words, to be a bodhisattva means to free ourselves in service to the well-being of others. The Buddha lived as a bodhisattva countless lifetimes before becoming a Buddha. This path is characterized by cultivating the Ten Perfections (the Paramis): generosity, ethical integrity, renunciation, wisdom, energy, patience, truthfulness, determination, kindness, and equanimity. I took bodhisattva vows early on in my Buddhist practice and, as a practice, they continue to serve as a moral compass for daily conduct and service.

In this practice, I have come to recognize the sacred geometry of the Ten Perfections at play in many spheres, including artistry.

For example, I have honored how my mother was a contemporary bodhisattva throughout her life through her artistry as a musician. On the third Friday night of each month, she'd hold improvisational jazz sessions. Because she played the piano, and a piano is not exactly portable, all the sessions took place at our house.

I remember my excitement while I was peeking out from the bedroom door. The other musicians would pile into our living room with their instruments: the bass fiddle, saxophones, trumpets, drums; a full range of African and Afro-Cuban percussionists. There were singers, too. These were business owners, politicians, the working poor, and the unemployed.

My mom would often hum a rhythm before expressing it on the piano and then everyone else would join in when they felt so moved—when they knew they could add value, meaning, interest, and harmony.

I'd be amazed at how everything was made more powerful in ensemble. There was a sense of complementarity, not competition, as if they knew they were in cocreation and that something subtle and mysterious was unfolding. These folks were playing for each other, and there was deep respect and trust in what unfolded. No one contributed just to be heard but rather to create something more beautiful.

The sounds each musician made were like statements and questions that the other musicians were affirming and answering, the very meaning of the questions expanding and changing in response. Every musician and singer would be highlighted at a certain time, but not with a solo in the conventional sense. It was more spacious and spontaneous—an inflection, a fragrance, a gradation, unassuming yet distinct.

Most of these folks could play music much better than they could speak, and they preferred it that way. No one had sheet music, and no one followed a script. The ears and heart were in charge. It was the listening and the emotion absent of words or reason that were on display. No one could make what was happening happen on their own.

What they created together could not be repeated, and it

wasn't meant to be. It was a gift in the moment—a gift of presence, genuine expression, exchange, and care. The musicians themselves were nourished and fortified, and everyone in their range was touched lovingly.

As I reflect on this mysterious and precious transmission through improvisational jazz, I realize that what is ripened in the practice of the Ten Perfections is similar to what is ripened in the creation of improvisational jazz; however, I would choose different words to describe it, such as tenderness, empathy, flexibility, curiosity, gratitude, respect, composure, and harmony.

The nature of art, in my mind, is collective. The discipline of an artistic practice concentrates the energy needed to cook an honest and tender response to well-being and truth. The Buddha was an artist through storytelling and poetry. Art births us into intimacy with life and offers the prospective for social harmony. Through art, we recognize that we are extensions of each other—reflections of the human heart.

The late, great American novelist Toni Morrison wrote, "I know the world is bruised and bleeding, and though it is important not to ignore its pain, it is also critical to refuse to succumb to its malevolence. Like failure, chaos contains information that can lead to knowledge—even wisdom. Like art."⁴ And as she wrote in her last book, *The Source of Self-Regard*, "Art reminds us that we belong here. And if we serve, we last. . . . [It's] critical to the understanding of what it means to care deeply and to be human completely."⁵

I ask myself daily, *As a bodhisattva, how might I see all life as art, as ceremony in service to greater well-being for all, without exception?*

Mindful of Race

Moving to the South amplified an unnamable upset deep within me. This upset, along with racial threat throughout the nation and the pervasive racial ignorance within dharma communities, ignited the need for deeper understanding and exploration of our relationship to race and racism. I was particularly interested in how we transform racism using the principles of Buddhism and the tools of mindfulness. For this reason, I chose to write a book about it.

That book, *Mindful of Race: Transforming Racism from the Inside Out*, examines structural racism and our role in it through a mindfulness lens and diagnoses racism as a heart disease that's curable. The book supports a deeper understanding of four common questions asked by spiritual seekers:

How do I work with my thoughts, fears, and beliefs in ways which nurture the dignity of all races?

How do I comfort my own raging heart in a sea of racial ignorance and violence?

How can my actions reflect the world I want to live in and leave to future generations?

How do I advocate for racial justice without causing harm and hate, internally and externally?

To further racial healing within Buddhist communities, I also used my professional background in diversity consulting and designed and began teaching the Mindful of Race training program. For the past several years, this program has supported individuals and groups across the nation in understanding and transforming racial habits of harm.

Core to this training is the formation of racial affinity groups, a mindfulness structure that deepens understanding and integration, allowing for a rare opportunity to live an experience dedicated to racial awareness and genuine connection with members of our own race, while also ripening our capacity to engage across race.

This training is my way of cultivating a path of racial literacy and well-being so that each of us can feel connected and more aware of our impact, as we do what must be done.

Teaching the Dharma

When I teach the dharma, my primary focus is to offer a way for practitioners to look at their mind to recognize what feeds freedom. My basic assumption is that they come to contemplate their lives through the lens of the dharma. The choice to work with their mind for a period of several days says to me that they want to understand suffering and its end, in this very moment—that they want to shift from being ensnarled in suffering to being curious about it, and to ride the waves of mind and body experiences *here and now* and *know for themselves* its nature.

Being a Black lesbian, great-grandmother, trained as a psychotherapist and diversity consultant, I'm not insensitive to power, trauma, race, or racism, the horrors of which will inevitably arise on retreat. But when I look at POC and Black folks in particular, I don't see us as fragile, wounded, or traumatized people needing special treatment. I see a force for good! Our ancestors came through many trials and tribulations; all of them experienced trauma. Trauma was a comma, not a period!

Many of our ancestors and wise elders set an example of strength, dignity, and resilience. Their unfinished struggles are transformed through our wise actions and service. And I believe our ancestors are giggling and celebrating our choice to be free in heart and mind.

In this seat, I am not focused on your story but on the direct experience *story* is having on this moment. I am more invested in your freedom than your comfort zone or safety, and I won't be complicit in your suffering. I'm listening intently to your rhythm of unfolding, how you are freeing yourself through the practice, and how you are contributing to improvisational jazz—a sound larger than self-interest or indulgence. My greatest joy in teaching is witnessing the dharma mature in my student's mind and heart.

Taking the teacher seat has not been a walk in the park. The context of Western dharma training is flooded in whiteness. Distinguishing my experience—pulling a black thread out of a tapestry of whiteness—has often felt overwhelming and self-doubting. Yet the dharma is deeper than race. Fundamentally, there is no way to teach the dharma without being taught by the teachings.

One way I stay grounded as a teacher is to remember the advice of an early mentor who advised me that I need to only do two things when I teach the dharma: (1) share what the Buddha taught and (2) share how you know it to be true from your direct experience. This simple humility practice supports me in distinguishing the interplay of thoughts and direct experience, knowledge and wisdom, and ego and truth. More importantly, staying close to the bare bones of direct experience allows me to bring the entirety of my life to the teachings and to be more creative in my expression of the dharma, which lately has included music and dance.

For me, teaching the dharma is art more than science; it's an emergent sharing of what's difficult and mysterious through direct insight, beauty, and love.

For Black folks in the dharma, our waves can be intense and engulfing like tsunamis: no one is exempt from their impact. It's important to remember that the Buddha specialized in freedom from suffering—something we can know directly and exemplify.

Throughout his life, the Buddha asked us to know the truth for ourselves. On his death bed, when so many felt faithless, he instructed all beings: "Be your own refuge. Have the dharma as a refuge. Make yourself a refuge to all beings."

So, like my mother, I pray, and I also practice, because, despite our best efforts, we don't live in an ignorance-free or hate-free zone. Our hearts will be broken and will heal. Every thought and action gives birth to something—why not have it be freedom?

My advice: Practice the dharma, then do your best. Grieve, rest, keep hate at bay, and join with others for contemplation and refuge. Don't get too far ahead of now. This moment is enough to digest. Sit, breathe, open. Don't be a stranger to moments of freedom that may be flirting with you. Allow distress to teach you how to be more human. Sit in the heat of it until your heart is both warmed and informed, then make a conscious choice to be a light.

CONCLUSION

The Buddha made it clear:

The way out of suffering is not denying the existence of suffering, but going through it. Suffering is not created by magic, but has discernible causes in the real world. The causal patterns that lead to suffering can be altered through eight path elements.

Put in this formula, Buddhism, as a way of life, offers easy-to-follow guidance that has the potential to be beneficial for ourselves and others, regardless of our racial, ethnic, class, gender, or religious identifications. Suffering, from a Buddhist perspective, is universal, and while we may not be able to change what we experience, we can change how we relate to our experience. The key is knowing that we have choice in how we relate to any experience.

An African American griot-liberative writer, James Baldwin, once said, "People who cannot suffer can never wake up, can never discover who they are." We agree. The point is not to intentionally heap suffering on top of suffering but to allow the suffering that exists to be transmuted through self-tenderness so that we may deepen in insight and know who we truly are. An African American Zen priest, Zenju Earthlyn Manuel, in her book *The Way of Tenderness: Awakening through Race, Sexuality, and Gender,* invites us to do what Baldwin invited us to do. Our book's contributors, in their vulnerability, took you on a tenderizing journey to understand suffering and the end of suffering. How do you feel now? Are you ready to go deeper?

The authors in this book explore trauma, belonging, healing, and transformation as they each wrestle with their suffering. They sometimes seek and sometimes stumble upon the Buddhist teachings as they follow the path to cultivate compassion, love, and freedom. They remind us that the trauma of being alive is messy and that the same mess can be used as ingredients in the recipe for a delicious life. No meaningful experience needs to be ignored, garbage waste becomes compost fertilizer, and our very waste is our homeopathy. When we acknowledge our own suffering and ability to heal, nondualistically, we see the necessity for embracing change and moving beyond limited ways of thinking. When deep in our suffering, we tend to think we are isolated and no one is suffering like us, but the Buddha taught that this way of thinking is a delusion. In other words, it's time to get real, and we have the dharmic formula to be realized and actualized even with the difficulties brought on while living as black in the United States.

Suffering, pain, and trauma hurts but also can awaken us, teach us forgiveness, and help us be compassionate, if we learn how to transmute those imprints for the good of others. We've learned that if we are to know the full measure of our humanity, our intention must be freedom for ourselves and for others. Our liberation project is collective.

Since the first gathering of African American Buddhist leaders that took place in 2002 at Spirit Rock Meditation Center in Woodacre, California, the second (called The Gathering) in 2018 at Union Theological Seminary in New York City, and the most recent (The Gathering II) in 2019 at Spirit Rock Meditation Center, many more African American Buddhist, dharmic, and secular mindfulness leaders have emerged throughout the country. Our collective also includes Africans and the African diaspora. On our dedication page, we highlighted African American dharmic authors who published books before ours. Just as we asked you to find the books of authors who came before us, we ask you to go online and find these leaders who attended the 2019 gathering, including:

Femi Akinnagbe
Joshua Bee Alafia
Noliwe Alexander (organizer)

Laurie Amodeo
Chimyo Simone Atkinson
Rachel Bagby
Leslie Booker
Martina Bouey
Karla Jackson Brewer
Eli Brown-Stevenson
Patrick Brown
Myokei Caine-Barrett (organizer)
Audrey Charlton
Thomas Davis IV
Alisa Dennis
Mabinti Dennis
Angela Dews
Lawrence Ellis
Jozen Tamori Gibson
Claudelle Glasgow
Marisela Gomez
Gloria Gostnell
JoAnna Hardy
Phil Hardy
Rashid Hughes
Amana Brembry Johnson
Kate Johnson
Solwazi Samuel Johnson
Sensei Alex Kakuyo
Shaka N. Khalphani
Ruth King
Gina LaRoche
Rhonda Magee
Zenju Earthlyn Manuel
Konda Mason (organizer)
Vimalasara (Valerie) Mason-John
Stacy McClendon
Satyani McPherson
Justin F. Miles

Lisa Moore
Rev. Seiho (Clear Peak) Morris
Nobantu Mpotulo
Lama Rod Owens
Ericka Tiffany Phillips
Allyson Pimentel
Rev. Sherrilynn (JyakuEn) Posey
Arisika Razak
Tuere Sala
Anouk Shambrook
Shanté Paradigm Smalls
Syra Smith
Rev. Willie Mukei Smith
Phoenix Soleil
Ralph Steele
Suryagupta
Jasmine Syedullah
Rima Vesely-Flad
Alice Walker
Larry Ward
Dolores Watson
Fresh "Lev" White
Rev. angel Kyodo williams (organizer)
DaRa Williams
Jan Willis
Sojourner Zenobia

We are growing in numbers because our lives are a testament to what is working. We carry on the African griot dharma storytelling literary liberative movement with the belief and experience that there is no true freedom until we support one another in being free.

NOTES

FOREWORD

1. Jan Willis, *Dreaming Me: Black, Baptist, and Buddhist* (Somerville, MA: Wisdom Publications, 2008), 160.
2. Charles Johnson, "A Sangha by Another Name," *Tricycle* (Winter 1999), accessed June 3, 2020, https://tricycle.org/magazine/sangha-another-name/.
3. W. E. B. Du Bois, *The Souls of Black Folk*, https://www.gutenberg.org/files/408/408-h/408-h.htm#chap14.
4. Ralph Ellison, "Richard Wright's Blues" (1945) in *The Collected Essays*, ed. John F. Callahan (New York: Modern Library, 1995), 129.

INTRODUCTION

1. Bessel van der Kolk, *The Body Keeps Score: Brain, Mind, and Body in the Healing of Trauma* (New York: Penguin Books, 2014), 21.
2. Pamela Ayo Yetunde, *Object Relations, Buddhism, and Relationality in Womanist Practical Theology* (Cham, Switzerland: Springer Nature/Palgrave Macmillan, 2018), 45.
3. Adapted from Laura van Dernoot Lipsky, *Trauma Stewardship* (San Francisco: Berrett-Koehler, 2009). See chapter 7, "Following the Five Directions."

CHAPTER 1: THEY SAY THE PEOPLE COULD FLY

1. Virginia Hamilton, *The People Could Fly: American Black Folktale* (New York: Knopf, 1993), 171.

2. Davíd Carrasco, "Toni Morrison among Us," *Harvard Divinity School Current*, August 6, 2019, https://hds.harvard.edu/news/2019/08/06/david-carrasco-toni-morrison-among-us.

3. M. Shawn Copeland, *Enfleshing Freedom: Body, Race, and Being* (Minneapolis: Fortress Press, 2010), 3.

4. Henry Louis Gates Jr. and Maria Tatar, *The Annotated African American Folktales* (New York: Liveright, 2018), 65–72.

5. Hamilton, *The People Could Fly*, 166–73.

6. Audre Lorde, "A Litany for Survival," in *The Collected Poems of Audre Lorde* (New York: W. W. Norton Press, 2000), 255–56.

7. "Trauma," American Psychological Association, accessed June 3, 2020, https://www.apa.org/topics/trauma/index.html.

8. Sonya Renee Taylor, *The Body Is Not an Apology: The Power of Radical Self-Love* (Oakland, CA: Berrett-Koehler, 2018), 58.

9. Tarana Burke, "The Inception," accessed June 3, 2020, https://metoomvmt.org/the-inception/.

10. Rosenna Bakari, "Black Quiet Noise: Breaking the Silence on Sexual Assault within the Black Community," *Journal of Black Sexuality and Relationships* 5, no. 3 (2019): 25–41.

11. Matthew Abrahams, "The Trauma Dharma," *Tricycle*, April 10, 2018, https://tricycle.org/trikedaily/trauma-meditation/.

12. John Makransky, *Guided Meditation*, Innate Compassion Training 2016. For more on Makransky and his work, visit https://foundationforactivecompassion.org/.

CHAPTER 2: THE DHARMA OF TRAUMA

1. Alice Walker, *The Way Forward Is with a Broken Heart* (New York: Ballantine Books, 2012), 217.

2. James Baldwin, *Notes of a Native Son* (Boston: Beacon Press, 1955), 159–75.

3. Spring Washam is the founder of Lotus Vine Journeys, which organizes two-week Buddhist-based ayahuasca retreats.

4. Steven Mintz and Sara McNeil, "Enslavement," Digital History, accessed February 14, 2015, http://www.digitalhistory.uh.edu/disp_textbook_print.cfm?smtid=2&psid=445.

5. For more information about this kind of trauma transference, see Joy DeGruy, *Post Traumatic Slave Syndrome: America's Legacy of En-*

during Injury and Healing (Portland, OR: Joy DeGruy, 2005) and Resmaa Menakem, *My Grandmother's Hands: Racialized Trauma and the Pathway to Mending Our Hearts and Bodies* (Las Vegas, NV: Central Recovery Press, 2017).

6. See James Cone, *A Black Liberation Theology* (Maryknoll, NY: Orbis Books, 1986) to learn more about liberation theology and Blackness.

CHAPTER 3: TURNING TOWARD MYSELF

1. Gayatri Chakravorty Spivak, "Acting Bits/Identity Talk," *Critical Inquiry* 18 (Summer 1992): 795.

2. Nalin Swaris, *The Buddha's Way to Human Liberation: A Socio-Historic Approach, Part I* (Nugegodam, Sri Lanka: Sarasavi Publishers, 1999), 10.

3. Toni Morrison, "Black Studies Center Public Dialogue, Part 2" (lecture, Portland State University, Portland, Oregon, May 30, 1975). Accessed June 3, 2020, https://www.wweek.com/news/2019/08/07/one-of-late-writer-toni-morrisons-most-famous-quotes-about-racism-came-from-a-talk-at-portland-state-university-listen-to-it-here/.

4. Audre Lorde, "Uses of the Erotic: The Erotic as Power," in *Sister Outsider: Essays and Speeches* (New York: Ten Speed Press, 1984), 57.

CHAPTER 4: BELONGING

1. Thich Nhat Hanh, "Please Call Me By My True Names." Accessed July 24, 2020, https://www.brookes.ac.uk/poetry-centre/national-poetry-day/thich-nhat-hanh--please-call-me-by-my-true-names.

CHAPTER 5: VOLUNTARY SEGREGATION

1. Pamela Ayo Yetunde, "Audre Lorde's Hopelessness and Hopefulness: Cultivating a Womanist Nondualism for Psycho-Spiritual Wholeness," *Feminist Theology* 27, no. 2 (January 1, 2019): 1761–94.

2. Dr. Martin Luther King Jr., "I Have a Dream," address delivered at the March on Washington for Jobs and Freedom, accessed May 20, 2020, https://kinginstitute.stanford.edu/king-papers/documents/i-have-dream-address-delivered-march-washington-jobs-and-freedom.

3. Bhikkhu Nanamoli and Bhikkhu Bodhi, eds., *The Middle Length Discourses of the Buddha: A New Translation of the Majjhima Nikaya* (Boston: Wisdom Publications, 1995), 223.

4. Frank Charles, ed., *The Thompson Chain-Reference Study Bible New King James Version* (Indianapolis: B. B. Kirkbridge Bible, 1997), 1369.

5. Pamela Ayo Yetunde, "Buddhist Non-Self as Relational Interdependence: An NTU-Inspired African American Lesbian Interpretation?" *Buddhist-Christian Studies* 38 (2018): 3433–36.

6. Pamela Ayo Yetunde, *Object Relations, Buddhism, and Relationality in Womanist Practical Theology* (Cham, Switzerland: Springer Nature/Palgrave Macmillan, 2018), 45.

7. Bhikkhu Bodhi, "Brahmasamyutta: Connected Discourses with Brahmas," in *The Connected Discourses of the Buddha: A Translation of the Samyutta Nikaya* (Boston: Wisdom Publications, 2000), 232–33.

8. I borrow the notion of magical and mythical and mystical from the religious philosopher Jean Gebser.

9. Emmanuel Y. Lartey, *Postcolonizing God: An African Practical Theology* (London: SCM Press, 2013), xvi.

CHAPTER 7: ON BEING LAILAH'S DAUGHTER

1. Gosho Translation Committee, "The Four Virtues and the Four Debts of Gratitude," in *The Writings of Nichiren Daishonin* (Shinanomachi, Japan: Soka Gakkai, 1999), 637.

2. Mos Def, "Umi Says," track 8 on *Black on Both Sides*, Rawkus and Priority Records, 1999.

3. Daisaku Ikeda, *Buddhism: Day by Day Wisdom for Modern Living* (Santa Monica, CA: Middleway Press, 2006).

4. Billie Holiday, vocalist, "Good Morning Heartache," by Irene Higginbotham, Ervin Drake, and Dan Fisher, Decca Records, New York City, recorded January 22, 1946.

5. Jae Nichelle, "Friends with Benefits," @ Write about Now Poetry (TGS 2017), October 31, 2017, YouTube, https://www.youtube.com/watch?v=1vKL5K_n6Zo.

6. Toni Morrison, *The Bluest Eye* (New York: Random House, 2007), 124–25.

7. Neel Shah, "Behind the Headlines about Maternal Mortality, Institute for Healthcare Improvement," last modified March 14, 2019,

http://www.ihi.org/communities/blogs/behind-the-headlines
-about-maternal-mortality.

8. Quoted in "Maternal Mortality: An American Crisis," CBS News, last modified August 5, 2018, https://www.cbsnews.com/news /maternal-mortality-an-american-crisis/.

9. Daisaku Ikeda, Words of Wisdom: Buddhist Inspiration for Daily Living, https://www.ikedaquotes.org/health-illness/health -illness203.html?quotes_start=7.

CHAPTER 8: WHOLENESS IS NO TRIFLING MATTER

1. Toni Cade Bambara, The Salt Eaters (New York: Random House, 1980), 1, 10.

2. Bambara, The Salt Eaters, 1, 10.

3. bell hooks, All About Love: New Visions (New York: William Morrow, 2001), 140.

4. Toni Morrison, "No Place for Self-Pity, No Room for Fear," The Nation, March 23, 2015, https://www.thenation.com/article/archive /no-place-self-pity-no-room-fear/.

5. Toni Morrison, The Source of Self-Regard: Selected Essays, Speeches, and Meditations (New York: Knopf, 2020), 53.

ABOUT THE EDITORS

CHERYL A. GILES, PSYD, is the Francis Greenwood Peabody Senior Lecturer on Pastoral Care and Counseling at Harvard Divinity School and a licensed clinical psychologist who teaches courses on spiritual care, trauma and resilience for caregivers, and compassionate care of the dying. Cheryl is a core faculty member of the Buddhist Ministry Initiative and coeditor of *The Arts of Contemplative Care: Pioneering Voices in Buddhist Chaplaincy and Pastoral Work* (Wisdom Press, 2012). She is on the board of directors at Barre Center for Buddhist Studies.

PAMELA AYO YETUNDE, JD, THD, is a Community Dharma Leader in the Insight Meditation community. She is also a pastoral counselor and professor of pastoral counseling, spiritual care, and chaplaincy. She is the author of *Object Relations, Buddhism, and Relationality in Womanist Practical Theology* (Palgrave Macmillan, 2018) and *Buddhist-Christian Dialogue, US Law, and Womanist Theology for Transgender Spiritual Care* (Palgrave Macmillan, 2020). Ayo has contributed essays to *Buddhadharma, Lion's Roar,* and *American Buddhist Women* magazines. Pamela Ayo Yetunde can be reached at www.centeroftheheart.org.

CONTRIBUTOR BIOS

GAYLON FERGUSON, PHD, is a senior teacher of Buddhist meditation in the lineage of Chögyam Trungpa Rinpoche. He is a core faculty member in religious studies at Naropa University and the author of *Natural Wakefulness* (Shambhala, 2009) and *Natural Bravery* (Shambhala, 2016). Gaylon is working on his third book, *Welcoming Our True Nature: The Revolutionary Wisdom of Beginner's Mind.*

REV. GYŌZAN ROYCE ANDREW JOHNSON currently resides at Auspicious Cloud Temple (Houston Zen Center). He continues the practice of awakening in all forms, together with all beings.

RUTH KING, MA, is an international meditation teacher in the Theravada tradition of Buddhism. She is on the teacher's council at Spirit Rock Meditation Center and Insight Meditation Community of Washington, DC. King is the author of several publications, including *The Emotional Wisdom Cards* (Sacred Spaces Press, 2010) and *Mindful of Race: Transforming Racism from the Inside Out* (Sounds True, 2018). King teaches the Racial Affinity Group Development Program and Mindful of Race training program to teams and organizations nationwide. Ruth King can be reached at www.RuthKing.net.

KAMILAH MAJIED, PHD, is a mental health therapist, clinical academician, and an internationally engaged consultant on inclusivity and contemplative pedagogy and practice. She has also practiced and taught Buddhism and mindfulness practice from several perspectives including mindfulness-based cognitive therapy, mindfulness, and racial justice, Buddhism and mental health, and mindfulness practices to preserve the environment. Majied gave opening remarks at the first White House Conference of Buddhist Leaders on Climate Change and Racial Justice, where she also facilitated a dialogue on ending racism among the internationally represented Buddhist leadership. Majied is on the faculty at California State University in Monterey Bay as a professor of social work.

LAMA ROD OWENS is an author, activist, and authorized *lama* (Buddhist teacher) in the Kagyu school of Tibetan Buddhism and is considered one of the leaders of his generation of Buddhist teachers. He holds a master of divinity degree in Buddhist studies from Harvard Divinity School. He is the author of *Love and Rage: The Path of Liberation through Anger* (North Atlantic Books, 2020) as well as a coauthor of *Radical Dharma: Talking Race, Love, and Liberation* (North Atlantic Books, 2016). Owens is the cofounder of Bhumisparsha, a Buddhist tantric practice and study community, has been published and featured in several publications including *Buddhadharma*, *Lion's Roar*, *Tricycle*, and the *Harvard Divinity Bulletin*, and has offered talks, retreats, and workshops in more than seven countries.

DAWA TARCHIN PHILLIPS is founder and CEO of Empowerment Holdings, an international mindful leadership development company and president of the International Mindfulness Teachers Association (imta.org), a professional trade organization for mindfulness teachers from twenty-seven countries. Dawa is a classically trained Buddhist *lama* (teacher) who completed six and a half years of deep meditation over the course of two consecutive three-year meditation retreats. Dawa teaches mindfulness and meditation, awakened leadership, and conscious business practices around the world. He is a resident teacher of the Santa Barbara Bodhi Path Center and a contributing author for *Mindful*, *Tricycle*, and *Lion's Roar*. His work has been featured in the *New York Times*, *Huffington Post*, *Men's Fitness*, *Forbes*, and *Fast Company*. You can learn more about him and his work at www.dawatarchinphillips.com.

SEBENE SELASSIE began studying Buddhism over thirty years ago as an undergraduate at McGill University where she majored in comparative religious studies. She has an MA from the New School where she focused on race and cultural studies. She is passionate about making the dharma accessible and relevant for our times by integrating the themes of belonging and identity into practice. Selassie is the author of *You Belong: A Call for Connection* (HarperOne, 2020).

"Wow! *Black and Buddhist* grounds meditation in naked truth-telling, showing that awakening to intergenerational rage and trauma liberates from the inside out. These searing accounts confirm the radical capacity of Black dharma teachers to show the way to freedom both ancient and now."—Judith Simmer-Brown, author of *Dakini's Warm Breath: The Feminine Principle in Tibetan Buddhism*

"There is richness here in texture, the individual awakenings that engage the senses and the heart—a response to the call of the ancestors walking with all their relations to guide and support the individual authors on their way home. Out of the depths of suffering are born love and joy, giving rise to the artistry of Blackness in all its forms. This journey into Blackness is a way of practicing the paramitas, underscored by the ever-present resilience and abundance of Black magic, of Black joy. Black folks have always known suffering—and have also always exhibited a wide array of ways to end suffering without sacrificing humanity, joy, or love. Accept the invitation. Be bathed in the warmth of Blackness. *Black and Buddhist* is a collection of dharma teachings that are profound and deep. This book will open your heart."—Myokei Caine-Barrett, Shonin Bishop, Nichiren Shu Order of North America

"The voices of our Black Buddhist sisters and brothers come as a unique gift that, as I hear them, lets me borrow from their courage, wisdom, and enduring hope. If we as a society are to move toward real health and well-being, let these voices of tested compassion and wisdom help lead the way!"—Bill Aiken, (retired) Director of Public Affairs, Soka Gakkai International—USA

"*Black and Buddhist* is a touching book of stories—a collective sharing of communal history, personal lives, and the threads that join us on the path to freedom from suffering. Wisdom comes through as each storyteller shares the impact of intergenerational trauma, what it means to live in a brown or black body, and how the dharma showed them a way to clear seeing and understanding."—Sharon Salzberg, author of *Lovingkindness* and *Real Change*